www.skylershah.co.uk

@SkylerShah #FullOfHappiness

Facebook.com/groups/APocketFullOfHappiness

www.skylershah.co.uk

@SkylerShah #FullOfHappiness

Facebook.com/groups/**APocketFullOfHappiness**

About The Author

Skyler Shah navigates the world of personal development uniquely. By swapping dull, template and superficial coaching, for engaging, energising and often experiential and adventure-based coaching, he creates *'unrealistic'* results with his clients who benefit from his varied trainings including NLP and Hypnotherapy.

Of his numerous careers he has enjoyed sharing on-track time with Olympic Gold Medallists, Piloting RAF Aircraft, International Modelling and working with Motorsport Champions.

In February 2015 his TEDx talk, *'Do something incredible, live your dream'* encouraged every listener to pick up a coloured pen and begin with happiness.

www.skylershah.co.uk

@SkylerShah #FullOfHappiness

Facebook.com/groups/**APocketFullOfHappiness**

A Pocket Full Of: Happiness

A guide to creating your own happiness, instantly

Skyler Shah

Wild Heart Publishing

Copyright © Skyler Shah, 2016

Skyler Shah has asserted his right to be identified as the author

of this Work in accordance with the Copyright, Designs and

Patents Act 1988

Published by Wild Heart Publishing, 2016

A catalogue record for this book is available from the British

Library.

Illustrations and cover design by Skyler Shah

www.skylershah.co.uk

@SkylerShah #FullOfHappiness

Facebook.com/groups/APocketFullOfHappiness

To Mum,

Your strength, determination, love and support continuously inspire me. Thank you.

www.skylershah.co.uk

@SkylerShah #FullOfHappiness

Facebook.com/groups/**APocketFullOfHappiness**

Table of Contents

A Pocket Full Of: Happiness   1

First Thing's First   4

The Truth Is, You Don't Really Want To Be Happy   11

I Am Really Bad At Making Decisions   20

A Light In The Darkness   29

"Happiness, I Choose You!"   32

How We Convince Ourselves We Are Powerless   43

I Don't Know What I Am Supposed To Do With

My Life   55

Dependency Issues And Idiots   65

Go Do Yourself   74

Feel Free To Say Anything   91

Que Sera, Sera   96

Taking The Ultimate Chill Pill   103

It's Nothing Personal   115

Worrying About Future Events That Haven't Hap-

pened And Might Not Ever Happen?   119

Thinking Life Into Existence	*130*
Today Is A Good Day To Die	*138*
That's Hardly Realistic Now, Is It?	*147*
There's Nothing Wrong With A Bit Of Self-Love	*162*
At The End Of The Day	*167*
On Your Bike	*179*
List Of Questions	*185*

www.skylershah.co.uk

@SkylerShah #FullOfHappiness

Facebook.com/groups/**APocketFullOfHappiness**

www.skylershah.co.uk

@SkylerShah #FullOfHappiness

Facebook.com/groups/**APocketFullOfHappiness**

A Pocket Full Of: Happiness

Hello! (You can say hello back if you like). I want to personally welcome you to this exciting *'Pocket'* book. In this edition you have the opportunity to explore how, in seconds, you can create your own happiness and carry that (along with this handy book) with you throughout your days.

Inside, you will find interesting insights and useful exercises to get you feeling deeply happy (we don't need any of that superficial stuff). And if the benefits stayed there that would be enough! But they don't. The gains from this book will impact every area of your life for the better.

You would be very wrong to assume that this is just another self-help book for people suffering from low-mood and depression. This wonderful little pocketguide can help anyone add to their current level of happiness; so low or high, prepare to feel happier.

You're about to go on a seriously great adventure. My name is Skyler Shah, and I will be your guide. Have your arms and legs wherever your heart desires and leave that part of your brain that's been keeping you safe, bored and understimulated, (we'll call that your *safety brain*), at the door. Today is the day you start having fun!

Welcome to your world of Happiness.

Fig 1: Draw your 'safety brain.'

First Thing's First
(Curious idiom wouldn't you agree? Talk about stating the obvious!)

Congratulations are truly in order before we even begin to get into the accessible depths of happiness. No matter what, simply because you have this book, simply because you are reading this book you have dramatically increased the opportunities available to you to live a happy and fulfilled life. That kind of dedication is greatly rewarded.

In addition to that, I want to add a few conditions before we begin so that you know you are doing the best that you can do to create your own happiness.

Condition number 1: *You lighten up.*

I don't care if you consider yourself a mead-swigging, tree-cuddling fairy elf; we can all, myself included, do with lightening up.

What this means for you is that you will read what you read with an open mind. You will do what you do with an open mind, and if you are the type of person who is predisposed to scepticism, consider this as your first all-encompassing experiment. An experiment where the methodology requires you to remain without scepticism, in order for the results to show the greatest accuracy; where the very moment you are sceptical and your mind closes, you eliminate the opportunity for a fair and unbiased result. Where your own beliefs, which will undoubtedly be geared negatively and against this working i.e. you not being happier, will come to fruition. You do not want this to happen.

Essentially, unlike the way in which we have been taught to analyse and moderate the world, instead of it being false until proven correct, make this experiment the reverse of that. Act 'AS IF' everything you read and do in and from this book is correct until it definitively, unequivocally and can, with 150% certainty be ruled out as incorrect. This does not mean by any reasoning however that I want you to blindly believe what is written. Your responsibility to yourself, me and those around you is to TEST everything, that way you'll gather your scientific evidence from which you can make well informed decisions and notice real results.

Remember, if you're not fully committed mentally, your results will resonate with that and they too will not give a fair and accurate representation of what is possible. One failure or one successful experiment is not enough to help you achieve 150% certainty. Test and retest. This is Condition one. Deal?

If this is a no deal by the way please close the book and leave, even if you are in your own house. Your house doesn't want to see you right now.

Condition number 2: *You engage fully.*

This means no half-arsed attempts or punts at making this work. That will not work, at least not in the long-term which I believe would be the outcome you are most interested in. If you are going to do this, do it properly otherwise when it doesn't work out the way you'd dreamed and imagined, you're going to prove yourself right and re-convince yourself that the world is just a dark place and you don't deserve to be happy. And in addition to that you read this amazing book with exciting and apparently effective exercises and EVEN THAT didn't work. There truly is no hope...

Don't be that person. It's a waste of everyone's time, yours, mine and the people you whinge to when it doesn't go the way you'd like. Give this your all, commit to being happy, "No matter what". Deal? (Same arrangement again, if it's a no deal, just leave).

Condition number 3: *Expect to feel happier, but don't necessarily expect to know what that actually feels like.*

Let's face it, most of the time if we actually kept track of how we felt, we wouldn't quite know how to label and categorise it. If we're not good and we're not bad, then by not being bad, does that mean we're good, and happy?

One of the ways in which we can make ourselves feel less happy and more depressed than we actually were before we started analysing it, is by comparing how we were to our expectations (and often our unreasonable expectations) of happiness. Yes happiness is amazing when it is the kind of body-trembling, euphoric, serotonin-pumping, face-crinkling experience we hold onto and remember on a rainy day. But, those experiences come as a result of extraordinary stimulation. Engaging as comprehensively as you possibly can with this book will do many things, but believing you will spend every minute of your life afterwards floating on a cloud of ecstasy is not in line with its purpose, though I am not saying at all that it cannot happen!

We will do check-ins to begin exploring and clocking your happiness gauge, but before we do that, you will benefit from spending a little time locking-down in your mind what exactly happiness is to you, and what it would look like and feel like for you to be at the baseline of your happiness.

I will add this exciting note onto this condition however. We are creating a consistent level of happiness in your life. The beautiful thing is when you are already happy, the opportunities to access higher levels of happiness are not only closer and more accessible, but they are more numerous and more frequent too. You really do bring towards you that which you give out. This is where the conditions end.

Consistently maintain agreement with these and you will witness your life change, and I can write confidently, that this is without doubt.

I have worked with many people over the years, and those who have gone from strength to strength, those who have made their lives something others dream of even witnessing; those are the ones who are committed to being open and fully committed, to experimenting with their own lives boldly, and who endeavour each day to create happiness, and lightness and an effortless flow that propels them with such lucid vigour into their amazing futures that any other way of being would simply be exhausting.

I would love to help you become a member of this extraordinary group.

The Truth Is, You Don't Really Want To Be Happy

This probably sounds like a load of old tosh, I mean, come on, you bought this book right, of course you want to be happy!

Except, there is a big part of you that really, really does not want to be; otherwise you would be.

Humans are canny creatures, we are smart, we are intelligent and everything we do we do on purpose, and we derive not only a benefit from that, but a perceived GREATER benefit from doing that opposed to doing other things, which is why we chose to do it in the first place.

I appreciate this is a curious topic that might quickly sound convoluted, so here is an example:

James wants desperately to be happy (or so he thinks), but James, like you is a bit of a muppet. What he believes will directly result in him being able to be happy is having a more concrete certainty that his job is secure. Knowing that his future is secure he can buy that house that he wants, and give the girl that he will find, once he has that amazing house, the best wedding the world has ever seen; and after having beautiful children, die peacefully together with his wife, spooning lovingly in his sleep at the ripe age of 100.

So each day James worries, and as each day passes his anxiety about his future increases, after all, not only does he not know about his future, but now he is finding it difficult to know about his future, could they be hiding something? Is he not smart enough to know? Is he getting closer to losing his job and spending the rest of his life in a cardboard box? Probably. And that will be as a result of the weirdo he has become by worrying about the things that he believes in discovering will make him happy.

As wild and dramatic as this story sounds, it may not

be far off a story you have created for yourself, and you will most probably know a person or two who has created something similar. And it doesn't stop there, the reasons to be unhappy are endless.

Some people carry guilt about past events and for them, the misery is a reminder or even a punishment for that, so God forbid they feel happy (even though they say they want to be).

Others use unhappiness as a motivation for success. They will spend their lives highly driven, trying their best to discover the happiness that others seem to live and breathe. In a bid to desperately scramble out of their hole, they will dig their way deeper and deeper to new and unprecedented successes; but the happiness that they are really working so hard to have is always a carrot on a string away.

Whatever it is for you, it is okay. Before I take this a little further and in a slightly different direction, I want to ask you two questions (Question 1 & Question 2). With each of these questions, once you have your first answer, I would urge you to challenge it and ask yourself, "Is this really THE answer? Is there something deeper than this?" This is where you begin to be incredibly honest with yourself. Proceed with candour. Elaborate. Give as much of yourself to this as you possibly can. Deal?

Think of something that is currently making you, or has recently made you unhappy.

Question 1: *What are the mental and real-world physical consequences of me being unhappy with this?*

(I.e. "Because I am unhappy with this, I respond/act/behave/feel/change/create situations such as 'x' which possibly and directly create 'y'." This is an example. Elaborate.)

Question 2: *How do I benefit from this?*

This is not a trick question. You are smart, you are driven and you are committed to living a happier more fulfilled life. Part of that is knowing that there are always benefits to doing what you do. What are *your* benefits for being unhappy?

Your answers to this may be very profound, deep and personal. It may appear to bring back memories of things you convinced yourself you had left behind, that in actual fact you may have been acting from and using to keep you living in a certain way, perhaps even unhappily.

For this reason, give yourself time and space to answer this question, but know that too much time and too much space can also be a means of avoidance. This book will support you through the changes you are about to experience. Be brave and where appropriate speak with others about your experience. There is no good in dealing with the things that might trouble you alone. And there is endless good to be had from sharing.

Question 3: *If instead of being unhappy I was happy, it would not be beneficial for me because it would mean...*

Very often, the benefit you discover to be behind the kind of actions that result in your unhappiness, those which we like to call actions of masochism and self-sabotage, are actually a means of self-protection or self-betterment.

For example: If your boss at work was being unkind, and you really let that affect you and after answering questions 1 to 3, you discovered that for you personally, you benefited from being unhappy because it reminded you to keep working hard so that you can take his job, well, that's certainly a positive to come from that. Likewise as a result, you may believe that if you were happy in that situation it would mean that you are just complacent and living a passive life and that you will probably amount to nothing special in the end. If that is not the way you want your life to go, making sure you are unhappy is certainly a good way to keep you from living that exact fear. However, without appropriate action, that may simply act as a friendly illusion whereby you think because you are not happy, you are on your toes.

It is possible to be equally as ineffective, complacent and passive at the same time as being unhappy, I can assure you.

But choosing to be unhappy in these ways isn't wrong. This isn't a 'bad ' way to be. It is a choice that you have intelligently made. The beautiful thing is however, that it isn't the only choice available to you, rather, it is just one of the easiest. And I would like to reiterate, choosing to be unhappy this way is perhaps no more or less effective than its, "Be happy and complacent" brother in achieving the purpose of active and intentional living.

Both, in the end, depend on you and what you decide to do i.e. the actions you take.

The difference between who, how and where you are right now and 10 minutes from now is not made in the choices and decisions you make, but in the actions you take.

Nothing will ever happen unless you take action. Better still, regular, consistent and directed action. That is why you have made the commitments at the beginning of this book. Because you want to change your life and become happier, and you know that doing so involves first, not just being prepared to change yourself, but taking action and doing it.

Fig 2: 'Create an image to represent all of the selling points (your benefits) to being unhappy. Make it bold and be creative. This is your space.'

I Am Really Bad At Making Decisions.
(What a Decisive Comment!)

I speak with many people who are more than forthcoming in telling me, or anyone who will listen in fact, that they are bad at making decisions.

This somehow apologetic statement is very useful for personal mitigation and encouraging others to feel a little softer (and maybe even) sorry for you, but in actual fact, that statement is really just a load of bulls***.

To begin with, in saying, "I am really bad at making decisions." You have yourself decided (even if based on information from others) that you are indeed bad at making decisions!

When we shift our attention to the biology and

functioning of your body we can see clearly how you are so immensely intelligent and highly tuned that even without realising, you are making decisions. To breathe in, to breathe out. Laugh all you like, life would be a great deal more difficult if you were bad at making these kinds of decisions.

And finally, when you experience any sort of stimulus, your brain fires lots of information around your head and generates ideas, thoughts, responses and emotions. Not only in the instant that you think something in your head have you decided that from all of the information floating around, *that* is the information for you. But if you communicate that in whatever way you do, be it blinking an eyelid, sign language or opening your mouth and speaking, YOU HAVE DECIDED to say what you say!

I want to ask you now. Are you actually bad at making decisions? I hope you have decided to change your mind.

So what do you really mean then? Most often, what that sentence means is, "I struggle to make decisions on things I feel have some sort of significance and/ or consequences affecting others."

Or, "I'm shy and don't like pressure/ people/ fearing I will make a 'bad' decision or a mistake, so I don't want to make a decision, and if I have to, forgive me for any errors I make and know that I will take a long time in making my decision."

If you have ever found yourself, and ever do find yourself thinking or expressing that you too are, "Bad at making decisions" you may find it beneficial to explore why that is for you.

Answer the questions below in as much detail and with as much honesty as you can. Let your mind run and your imagination go wild. If for you that is creating an extraordinary narrative where you become a billionaire, write it down.

Question 4: *What difference would it make, from today, if I no longer believed that I was bad at making decisions?*

Question 5: *What are my reasons for why, this time, I have chosen to believe that I am bad at making decisions? How does this belief benefit me?*

Question 6: *What exactly am I afraid of happening as a result, or in the process of confidently making a decision?*

Perhaps it is one of the above examples, perhaps it is something else or a variation of them. The great thing about this exercise is that in exploring the frames that you are using to build these stories, you will find *'flags'* and *'signposts'* to areas that you would do amazingly at growing in, and more than that, accepting.

I want to use this moment to remind you that it is okay to be afraid. As an animal and as a human it is natural to have fears. These questions are for your use to explore what exactly it is that you are afraid of so that should you choose to continue on this pathway to creating your own happiness, you can start to shine a light on them and let them be seen. You may choose and decide that you would rather not stop being afraid of them after they are uncovered and for whatever your reasons, take action and continue to fear them. And right now that would be okay because simply by doing so will you have owned more of your life and what happens in it. You would be choosing to be afraid and choosing to have that fear influence your actions. That kind of personal accountability is vital in maximising your happiness, though to really be as happy as you believe possible, functioning from fear is not the most effective way to achieve that.

Limiting beliefs are often based upon the expectancy and prediction of a pivotal negative event that you fear happening, and therefore are choosing to avoid. You may find questions 7, 8 and 9 relevant at various other points in this book, and though incredibly important, their obviousness can sometimes result in them being taken for granted.

Question 7: *What is the worst-case scenario possible as a result of me not acting on my belief that I am bad at making decisions?*

And;

Question 8: *What is the best-case scenario possible*

as a result of me not acting on my belief that I am bad at making decisions?

Question 9: *What is the most probable outcome of me not acting on my belief that I am bad at making decisions? And how terrible, really, would that actually be in the scope of the entire wonderful life I have yet to live and create?*

The 'happiness' you're creating all depends on you. At the end of it all it is a choice you are going to make in answer to the question:

"Despite everything I know, feel and understand about this situation, do I choose to take action in line with feeling happy, or do I want to hold onto the stories I currently believe which, while making me relatively unhappy, keep me comfortable in this uncomfortable homoeostasis?" Because the answers to questions 7, 8 and 9 only do half the job.

Now you know to what extent you actually, logically believe you need to feel afraid to the degree where you willingly sap your own confidence.

The likelihood is that it's nowhere near where you thought originally, but in order to create happiness here, you are going to have to take action. Which way, from this moment, are you going to live?

The proof is in the pudding. The difference is in the action. It's your call.

Fig 3: Draw the worst-case and best-case scenario to a situation that you are apprehensive about in your life where you will be making a decision.

A Light In The Darkness

An interesting insight I would like to share with you is that sometimes, and often most of the time, the pathway is clearest in the darkness.

We try to know happiness so that we can better create it, and recreate it. We try to analyse it when we're in it and work out what happens when we are experiencing it. Chances are that the *thing or things* that you currently believe hold the key that happiness, whatever this *thing or things* are for you, from securing business deals to living intense moments of passion or joy, is something you believe you have little or a rarity of. In this case it may be useful to look not towards the things you don't have a lot of and would love, but in the direction of what you believe wholeheartedly you have a bounty of, and begin to 'know' that place. You'll have a greater history and experience of it and have more numerous resources to access it.

Giving yourself a moment and some space to be where you are in the *'bad'* times will help you to realise more clearly how you feel and think to what is happening in those moments, and perhaps know better why you are responding in that way. You then have a pretty comprehensive action plan of things you want to do differently and things you no longer want to do and experience at all.

Why this is important is because the more you understand that you are in control of yourself, and thus your own life; the more accountable you are to yourself and the more power you realise you have access to in changing your life.

Think now to one specific negative thought or emotion you are currently experiencing or you have recently experienced, and ask yourself:

Question 10: *What does it mean about who I am and how I am right now, that I felt/feel, thought/think, responded/respond how I did/do? What else does it mean? (Keep asking that tag question until you feel you truly have nowhere else to go.)*

Tip: Be self-compassionate. It is easy to look to how you have responded to things and just say, "Well, it's clear I'm just a selfish ape." But instead, what will serve you better is to explore what that selfishness meant to you, why you believe you might have acted in that way, and explore where that shows you that you would benefit in growing and how you can become a better, more comfortable and happy version of yourself today.

"Happiness, I Choose You!"
(For those of you who, like me, found endless happiness in Pokémon as a child)

The first talk I ever delivered in the field of personal development was on *'Choice'*. I had asked myself, "What is the most powerful thing someone can take away with them in a talk of under two hours?" And concluded that it would be the practical knowledge of accountability and the key to regaining ownership of their lives.

I'd booked the room and waited half an hour with my then girlfriend. I'd gone to the toilet and came out to see a young couple looking rather lost, I thought I'd offer them directions and soon discovered that they were there to see me.

Within the space of an hour and a half, these two

individuals and in fact my girlfriend of some years said that their lives had changed and they had learnt so much about themselves.

The couple left this feedback on my website a little while afterwards:

"Me and my partner attended one of Skyler's sessions. Firstly it was great and completely eye opening. Secondly I certainly believe more people need to know what he teaches! Me and my partner now use the knowledge which we learnt that day in our everyday lives. We now say to each other when we become doubtful or discouraged... Remember what Skyler said."

In this section I want to explore some of the ideas that I share in my talks on *'Choice'*, but also invite you to participate in some new exercises.

Everything that you do and experience and as a result

the way that you experience it, is the result of your choices.

The fact is, you are more powerful than you may have ever even imagined!

The list below may make you feel things, and if it does, take note and use those *'flags'* for your benefit. Remember Condition 1 and stick with this:

- *Every thought you will have and have ever had is a choice, that is something that you have created.*

- *Everything you ever do and will have ever done is the direct result of a choice that you have made, and again, that is something that you have created.*

- *Every feeling you will feel and have ever felt is something you have chosen to feel.*

Though many of the things associated with these three

bullet points may seem to be passive and involuntary; they are all the result of you and what you are creating of the world, how you create your own world and indeed see it.

As a consequence, all of the amazing and wonderful things that you can recall from your life will in some way be because of you. The amazing trip you had with your family when you were younger is something only you have experienced in the way that you have, because of the thoughts that you thought and the things that you did while you were there. If you left the room, decided you wanted to leave altogether, or were in a different mood, you would have experienced it all very differently.

It also means that too, as well as all of the wonderful things that you have experienced in life, you are also accountable for the not so wonderful things.

At the very root of this idea is emotion. It is after all

how we navigate our lives. If we are not using physical cues such as, "I'm hungry" and, "Oww that hurts" we are functioning from an emotional platform. Again, emotions that you have chosen to feel.

To subdue any anger or frustration that you may be feeling right now, I want to colour this for you.

I also want to remind you that the purpose of this chapter and challenging you to become 100% accountable for your life is to help you to take back control of your life and put the power in your hands, and that happens as a result of the uncomfortable adoption of the responsibility for your own life; past, present and future. Even with things that don't seem to be because of you, where you can't work out how on Earth it could be your *'fault'* (let's try and keep away from using that term though) just take it. Sometimes things that are, are, even when being the Einstein that you are, you can't understand how exactly that may be.

The moment you are willing to take responsibility for what you believe are all of the great, and all of the awful things that have happened to you in your life will be the moment you can really sit in the driving seat and make every second thereafter count in the way that you want it to. This is not necessarily an easy process and you will start to discover many uncomfortable areas where you really don't want to own your life. Use these 'flags'. Perhaps some of these markers will show you areas where you have limited yourself. Perhaps those areas are being used as a template for how you are living today.

I want to share this example with you to offer a clearer idea behind this way of thinking, a way of thinking I would like to remind you under the Conditions of this book that you have committed to living into.

In Western cultures we consider death (particularly of a loved one) to be a terrible, horrendous ordeal of loss; one in which we feel emotionally obliged through social conditioning to grieve deeply for a very long time. The body of our loved one too is important, for even with beliefs of spiritual detachment from the body, we want their remains to be cared for and looked after as we would if they were alive. When we lose somebody, we don't consciously think, "Well, they have died, now I can choose to feel sad or choose to feel happy." Simply by living in the place that you do, with and around the people that you do, learning and engaging with the ideas that you do, you have made your choice on how you will feel. Responding the way you do simply means that on some level, you have decided it is the correct way to respond in that given situation. Again, you are smart. You do not act involuntarily to life. You have a brain and a personality and your responses to life evidence that.

Now, if we look towards the cultural habits in the East, particularly for this example to Nepal, we see that their relationship with death is very different. Of course they still mourn and grieve, but they also have a very solid belief that the soul of their loved one keeps living. They believe that their soul is well and healthy and happy. This provides much comfort in this time of 'loss' knowing that actually, the thing they loved hasn't really died.

The body of their loved one is then taken to the top of a mountain where it is cut into palatable pieces for scavenging animals and provides ample food for everything from bacteria to vultures, who gratefully strip the skeleton of its nutrients.

To a Westerner, this is probably a horrendous thing to think of happening to their family member and they would most likely get upset and suffer psychologically for the rest of their remaining life as a result. But realistically, physically, it doesn't really make a difference, does it, what happens to the body.

In both situations, a loved one has passed away and their body has been disposed of. The same physical things are happening, the only difference is how those involved have chosen to respond emotionally (again even though this may, particularly at the time, not feel like a choice.)

Whether or not you understand this, or even right now believe this is very much beside the point. You are here to learn how to create even more happiness in your life, and you have committed to engaging with this book wholeheartedly to do just that.

By taking ownership and becoming accountable, coupled with knowing now that you have the power to make a difference directly to how you can respond to what you experience in your life, you will feel more in control more of the time. That, with practice, will result in you creating your own happiness.

I wrote *'in time'* because it is something you are going to experiment with and practice. Simply being able to wholeheartedly believe that you are accountable for everything that you feel, think, say and do is a skill, one which you are not currently trained in.

As with learning any new skill, it will feel uncomfortable. It will feel wrong. It'll feel like you're doing it wrong. And you'll feel like you want to quit and you will begin to convince yourself it doesn't work to justify that.

You made a commitment. Keep it. Your experiment is this.

Experiment 1:

To believe wholeheartedly, before proof and without doubt, that I am accountable for my own life. My thoughts, feelings, actions and the experiences in my life are directly accountable to me. I have that much power.

Fig 4: Now that you are accountable for your own life, past, present and future, draw a snapshot from the amazing life you will lead.

How We Convince Ourselves We Are Powerless
Powerless
(Because sometimes, the excuse is comforting)

I love language. It is at the centre of human existence and communication, and no matter how sophisticated the communication, is important in impacting your life and the lives of those around you. Even smoke signals have their unspoken meanings, like, "HELP, the beans overcooked and our camp is on fire."

But spoken language, or language communicated as if spoken, in particular is an exciting place to begin exploring for me because everything that we say and hear is all part of our reality. It directly informs how we understand our world. It is also something that many people take for granted; and on a daily basis use to grind themselves down so much that by the end of each day they feel deflated, depressed and done with the world!

I want to share with you how your choice of linguistics could be impacting your happiness, and offer some simple yet impactful solutions.

How many times today have you said or thought that you *'have to'* do something?

- "I have to pick up the kids", "I have to do the dishes", "I have to get something to eat."

And what about, *'need to'*. How many times has that little guy flopped out of your mouth?

- "I need to get that sorted", "I need to send that email" "I need to sort my life out!"

These sayings aren't uncommon, though you may not

until now have realised how often you or those around you have been using them.

I want to make this clear, there is nothing wrong with saying things like this. There's no need to go and give yourself fifty lashings. But there is a direct impact on how saying things these examples makes you feel and behave, and it is up to you to decide if your responses to these words are what you actually wish to have in your life.

In the last chapter we explored a little about how what you feel, think and how you behave are at their core based upon your choices. We also had a little look at how different cultures deal with death, and while it may be a choice to feel, think and behave the way you do, when it is in agreement with your culture and so something deeply integrated into your life, it may be difficult to change. With examples such as this, where the stimulus has such a powerful response with you;

instead of attempting to change the response, you can limit, and in some cases even completely cut out the stimulus and replace it with something a whole lot more favourable.

This is where we have some fun with linguistics. You are going to begin to reprogram your mind with linguistic alterations.

To begin, you will need to know exactly where you are at right now. I want to invite you to deeply analyse your own responses to certain phrases. Give yourself a moment to actually stop and understand what such phrases mean to you. Ready?

The first phrase I want you to respond to is, 'have to'. How does that phrase make you feel, think and want to behave?

It may help you to write these down so that you can

focus on your responses wholly and not dedicate a small percentage of your brain to remembering.

Perhaps put the phrase, *'have to'*, into sentences you are familiar with. Repeat it until you have a firm understanding of how you resonate with it.

Once you have a list of the ways that phrase encourages you to feel, think and want to behave, begin to explore how the phrase, *'need to'* makes you feel, think and want to behave.

Of course, I won't know exactly what's on your list of answers. If however it says "Murder someone", I'd strongly advise you to visit a doctor as soon as you can.

For most people that I have worked with, this exercise highlights a pressure. Almost as if there is some invisible enforcer or prison guard making them do things against their will. As if there is a gun to their head and they are being made and forced to do the dishes, take the bins out, wash the car etc.

This might be similar to your response, but at the end of it all, there is no gun, I hope! Just you and your decision as a smart and intelligent person that washing the dishes is the best thing for you because you recall that time a few years ago when you didn't, and the blue-green slime built up on the plates and stunk the house out of cheese.

In this rather convoluted way, you actually want to do the dishes. Moreover, you have chosen to do the dishes. You are back in the driving seat again.

So why have you created an invisible police officer to tell you that you have to? Probably because you don't enjoy doing the dishes. There are a million other things you would enjoy to do more, and so you need a serious reason to do the things you're not such a fan of.

The fact is, you are so powerful, that you have created this imaginary force that consistently makes you do stuff you don't believe you want to do, and certainly don't enjoy.

Just think about that for a moment.

For years, you have been doing stuff you don't want to do, because you have been telling yourself and you believe whole heartedly that you have had to do it. It's curious then to think of all of the things that you believe that you would or could enjoy doing, that you never do. Imagine if you used that incredibly powerful and convincing side of you to actually get you to take action and do those things that you would love. How amazing could your life be then?

You don't need to employ any tricks or to reassign the 'enforcer' to the 'enjoy' side of the brain. It always has been and always will be all you.

You may have noted in your personal response list that for you, *'have to'* is a negative thing. You wouldn't usually say, "I have to go and have an amazing dinner with my loved ones."

More likely you would say, "I am going to", and if it is not yet organised, "I want to".

You could, now that you know all of this, decide to have a little swap. Use *'have to'* for things you want to do, and use *'want to'* with things that actually you're doing because you believe they *'have to'* be done. And this may work for you, but I would advise against this. That negative pressure of not having a choice and, *'having to'* do something immediately detracts from your autonomy and accountability. Instead, know that you are in control, and whatever you are doing that deep down, somewhere, you want to do that.

Let's look at, *'need to'* now. You may have found some

similarities between the two phrases I asked you to explore. Both are formed on the basis of necessity and having no other choice. Here too you can replace 'need to' with 'want to' and eliminate the nasty feeling you might get with it, leaving you feeling happier knowing that you will do what you will do because you have chosen to.

Experiment with replacing your 'need to' and 'have to' with 'want to', and where you would normally use 'want to', keep that the same. Notice the difference it makes for you and after a while and some testing if it feels right, you can make the decision to keep it!

Wonderful I hear you shout, but what about doing the things I want to do that I don't do because I am 'too busy' doing the stuff I 'have to' do?

Simple, and this is your next experiment.

Experiment 2:

You have just discovered how incredibly powerful you are, having tricked yourself for so long into doing things you didn't enjoy. Now it's your time to open the flood gates to enjoyment in life.

Create a list of 50, yes 50, things that you would love to do, big or small. Structure each list item like this.

"I want to 'X' because 'Y' and it would mean 'Z'."

Get excited by this list, and once it's done put it somewhere you will see it each day.

Now here's where your life goes crazy. Choose one and do it. If it's a big one, work out your baseline requirements to do it i.e. skills, research, money etc and by what date at the earliest they can all be achieved. You now have yourself a date and an action plan. This is just as important as all of the things that you used to say you *'had to'* do. This is what makes all of those things worth it. This is living.

Fig 5: Draw your new relationship with your invisible enforcer.

I Don't Know What
I Am Supposed To Do With my Life
(Neither do I)

I have known many people who have swung in and out of depression as a result of questions like, "What am I supposed to do with my life", "What is my purpose" and the old favourite, "What is the purpose of life." And I have in the past been a member of this group.

It is a toughy because there really is no single definitive answer and you will challenge any answer you do get to a death match, and you will always win.

I recall crying on two different occasions in my teens at a time where I was due to choose my college subjects. It was an incredibly frustrating experience for me. I felt like I had so many skills in a variety of places. I had so many things I enjoyed for a range of different reasons and there were also so many things that I was yet to try and experience that the idea of choosing a set of subjects that would filter my life was heart-breaking. And then the year after that, deciding upon the four subjects that I would then use to decide my future. Wow, did I have a breakdown then.

Making decisions, concrete decisions about things that you believe have such importance can be very tough indeed. It has at many points plagued me to the point of frustration and tears. But it doesn't have to be that way.

The reason why these important decisions are so hard, so exhausting, and are such a point of distress and unhappiness in our lives is because we are being asked to think of a time other than now. To project into the unknown, then partly create a 'known' in making your decisions and hope that the things that happen during that time agree with your ideas. But let's face it, the future is an enigma, two seconds from now a monkey riding a panda bear could hover down the street, lasso you and take you to outer space to meet its fairy king. ANYTHING could happen (ask any quantum physicist).

So we are, in this decision making point, being asked to decide our future when we can't see past lunch time's cheese and bacon bagel offer, how we are supposed to do this is a mystery.

What if at the end of the year after making some important life decisions you hated doing one thing, decided that the other was not for you, you fell in love, and developed a passion for ancient Mongolian architecture? Would your year have been wasted? Would you be stuck on a path you didn't want to be on? Could you have made the 'wrong' decision?

I use 'wrong' loosely, and I will come to why shortly, but the answer to these questions are within you. The truth is, you do not know what your future holds. Even if you do a degree in a subject, it doesn't mean that you will become what you have studied to become. A year in a job, a weekend away, a chance meeting could send you in an unimaginably different direction. Simply because you have chosen to work in an office for 15 years does not at all negate your potential to become an explorer of the Amazon. Anything truly is possible, and your actions whether with volition or not result directly in that future.

So, if anything is possible, at any point. Are any decisions important? Well yes. The decisions you make, and your resulting actions directly impact your life. Making well informed decisions can lead you towards specific directions. If for example you decided you wanted to experience being an actor. Relocating to a small village where you work in an office at home and rarely get out of the house might not be the most effective pathway for you.

What you can take from this however, is that nothing

is permanent. Take for instance the atoms that make up your body. Sometimes they're there, sometimes they're somewhere else and replaced by other atoms that could have been making up a delicious pear 5,000 miles away. Nothing is permanent.

Feel free to take the pressure off now. I want to take you back to the question of whether you can be *'wrong'* in your decisions. A good friend of mine once told me, "Do what makes you happy". We can't be happy in the future, that only exists in our imaginations, right? So what if you chose to do what made you happy today (of course providing that doesn't result in the hurt or harm of others) and you made your actions based on that. This isn't to say spend all of your money on sky diving lessons and deprive your family of fresh water and nourishment; remember that maintaining your commitments to them will also make you happy, even if that is simply because you will not be moaned at by your hungry and dehydrated cohort.

Question 11: *If from today you chose to do what made you happy, in what ways could you not be making the 'wrong' decision?*

Question 12: *If from today you chose to do what made you happy, in what ways might you be making the 'wrong' decision?*

Question 13: *What could be possible if instead of trying to 'know' what to do with your life, you decided to 'be' in your life and by doing so, made each moment great for you?*

Question 14: *Imagine you have a completely clean and fresh canvas as your life. What would you love to do with it?*

The answer to this may not be wholly applicable, not everyone does have a completely clear canvas. But perhaps you do, and this question might just be the beginning of a very exciting adventure for you.

If your canvas isn't that clear, you still have choices.

Question 15: *What, from your vision in question 14, can you bring into your life today to help you begin that process of living into your dream?*

Even small changes from this place can result in exceptional boosts in happiness and once that ball starts rolling, you won't want it to stop. Better still, those around you will want to hop on too and the happiness that you created will spread.

One of the reasons why this exercise ends here for

many people is because of a lack of commitment. Changing something in their life sounds scary and disruptive and like a lot of effort, even if the results could be amazing.

That however, with your commitments to the Conditions in this book is not a concern I have of you.

Another reason why you may have left this exercise at the door is because of your own limiting beliefs. Heck, this stuff isn't new to you, you've probably always known deep down what you would love to do. It's just that there have been even more convincing excuses and reasons that have pulled the blanket over the door, even before you got to know the door was there and that the blanket existed.

Change after all is a scary thing, isn't it? It challenges the norms and everything that you are living in now. And though, right now might not be the best, right now you are alive, and you can't guarantee that with new fancy ideas. But then can you ever guarantee that?

The biggest challenge facing you right now might be selfishness. It might be that you don't want to be, or seem selfish by investing in yourself and living your dream. But would those around you not love to see you truly happy and fulfilled? Would you not be a greater role model and a nicer person to be around as a result?

If not selfishness, then loss is up there with the reasons why, if you hadn't made the commitments you had to this book, you might be likely to back off from an extraordinary life and settle into the comfortable uncomfortable swathe of your dull and trusty armchair.

If you changed and became happier, more in tune with who you were or decided you wanted to do different things with your life, how would that impact your relationship with your partner or friends? Would you drift apart, would you or they find someone else they're better suited to who made them happier? (would that really be terrible?) Would living your dream mean leaving something you cared for behind? These questions are best coupled with the two below. The answers to which should provide you with the confidence in yourself to continue with vigour and courage.

Question 16: *Am I prepared to love myself, to live congruently to who I am, even if it means that the relationships, things and people I love right now might change either by improving or ending, which too will be an improvement?*

Question 17: *Am I prepared to love those around me*

enough to let them experience me at my greatest and happiest, and love them no matter how they respond to that?

Find it in yourself to create a yes to both of these, and you'll fly.

Dependency Issues And Idiots
*(*87% of you will believe that title was about you. **That percentage was made up)*

It is almost impossible to be happy when feeling anxious. And perhaps you may have read the title of this chapter and felt anxious that it was about you. If you did, get over it and read on!

Before we begin, I want to be clear with you on what

my definition of anxiety is:

"Negative cognitions about future (and therefore imagined) events that have not yet (and might never) happen."

This differs from feelings of depression which while sharing a common theme in negative cognitions is more greatly affected by hopelessness. Often a feeling of lack of control and ability to affect a situation or your own future.

Though this book isn't specifically designed with the dissolution of depression in mind, many areas such as accountability exercises and experiments that demonstrate your ability to create change may be very positive in that capacity.

Please don't for a second think I am humouring these issues. Depression and anxiety affect many people in profound and often devastating ways. I have known both personally, and recognise the choke-hold that they can have on you. At the same time, one of the worst things you can do is put that label, *'depression'* or *'anxiety'* high on that god-like podium, making it bigger, more dominant and more in-control of you and your life. With depression in particular, this perpetuates the process of feeling hopeless, and things from that point without counter-action will only get worse.

Increasingly, it is becoming a social norm to be anxious about making a *'bad'* or *'wrong'* decision. It is then a place of great unhappiness, and something you can alter to drastically change your wellbeing and happiness for the better.

In some situations, like on the television game show, 'Who Wants To Be a Millionaire' for instance, there is one definitive right answer and three wrong answers to each of the 15 questions. These situations do exist outside of the land of television too, but are actually less obvious than you might imagine. In order for anything to be *'wrong'* there has to be a relationship, that is, something cannot be wrong without a specific scenario or context.

Squeezing out an almighty fart may not be appropriate and therefore *'wrong'* at your in-law's dinner table, but, at a fart party where the winner of the party games is the one who evacuates their rectal methane in the loudest fashion, doing so may just make you a champion.

There has to be a situation or a context in order to be *'wrong'*.

A common worry is that people want to choose the *'right'* path, and not be on the *'wrong'* path in their life. They don't want to make the *'wrong'* decision. If you refer back to the previous chapter, you can take solace in knowing that doing the *'wrong'* thing could simply mean doing that which does not make you happy.

If that doesn't agree with you, this is where you consult with yourself and discover what framework and context you are actually working from. It is very simple to say you don't want to do the *'wrong'* thing, but:

Question 18: *What actually would doing the wrong thing look like to you?*

Question 19: *How would you know it was the 'wrong' thing?*

And;

Question 20: *What are the definitive guidelines for you that in agreeing with, you would be doing the 'right' thing?*

Once you start playing this game and identifying the relationship/context of what you are basing your perceptions of 'wrong' and 'right' on, you will start to realise how often you actually don't face being 'wrong' at all, and how your expectations of how to be 'right' involve insane superhuman abilities such as seeing into the future and vague ideas like, "I want to take the 'right' path where I will become wealthy" (What is wealthy? How would you like to do that? When by?)

Other scary situations we find ourselves in, other than risking being 'wrong' include having no choice by 'needing' something. We say we 'need' many things, but actually, if we are outcome free, we don't need anything at all. Not even air unless (and here is the relationship) we wanted to live.

Technically, you don't need anything. You want to live and as a consequence, you 'need' air.

Idiots:

I mentioned in an earlier chapter that you, like everyone else, are smart and intelligent. At least, smart and intelligent enough to do what you believe is best for you; humans are not idiots, though they may often seem to act like it, and as such, we never actually make a *'bad'* decision.

Again, we worry we are going to make *'bad'* decisions in the same way that we worry about making *'wrong'* decisions. And as with being *'wrong'* or *'right'*, in this context at least, a *'bad'* decision can only exist within a framework. Someone murdering someone is bad in the framework of our culture and society. Someone eating a newly-wed's cake before they had a chance to try it is bad etiquette and morally a bit sketchy too, but, outside of that context it is what it is. It is just something that someone is doing.

More to the point, it is something that someone is

doing that they believe beyond all reasonable doubt is the best thing to do.

No one person has ever woken up and said, "You know what, today I am going to do the absolute worst for me, everything against my own personal interest." And if they had done that, on some level, taking those actions of sabotage were actually the best thing for them and exactly what they (deep down) believed they needed.

Your basic instinct is self-preservation and self-betterment. You will never make a *bad* decision ever again. If your decision doesn't work out for others, it's just not in line with their expectations. If it didn't go to your plan and doesn't work out for you, the real event wasn't in line with your expectations and also remember, it was the way you believed would best achieve your desired outcomes.

As a result, you can never do the *wrong* thing ever again. Yippee!

Fig 6: Draw your yippee moment.

Go Do Yourself

(They were trying to help you all along)

Wonderful, so right now you have a couple of experiments running. You've altered the way you're responding to what you're reading, you've adapted your linguistics, you are being more personally insightful and you can never be wrong. Sounds perfect, no?

Well I would like to believe that by now, some of the things you have been working on will have lifted you a little, but actually, we're not there yet. Unless you do this bit, you will always have a cap on the maximum amount of happiness you're going to be able to access.

In February 2015 I delivered a TEDx Talk titled, "Do Something Incredible, Live Your Dream". In that talk I explored how you can live your dream, and how that began (in my method anyway) with happiness.

One of the fundamental ways to begin creating your own happiness, is to be congruent to who you are, which first requires you to know who you actually are. Easier said that done, right?

Realistically, how often do you give yourself any time to actually stop and have a check-in to identify how you are feeling and what you really want?

I want to ask you a question:

Question 21: *What is your favourite colour, right now?*

(You may be very quick to give an answer. Give yourself time and space to make sure that right now, the colour you have chosen really is your favourite colour in this specific moment.)

It may sound like a very silly question to you. It may even sound irrelevant, and perhaps if you are thinking anything other than about your answer to the question right now, you are greatly skilled at avoiding being present with yourself, and as such could benefit even more from engaging fully with this exercise.

Once you have your colour, read on.

As I write this to you, my favourite colour is gold. The kind of honey coloured gold, with little glittery flakes in it. You know, if you were interested.

Ask yourself the following questions and again, give yourself space and time or as Einstein would say, spacetime, to make sure your answers are true to now. This is you creating a moment to slow things down, take a deep breath and get really present. This is not a race and the faster you whip through it, the more pointless it may seem.

What did I notice about my colour? Has it changed? If so, from when? Has it stayed the same? Did I immediately have an answer? Did this answer change when I challenged it? Why, right now, is it my favourite? How does my colour make me feel at this moment in time?

The reason for this question and the additional sub-questions is to bring you into the here and now. To not only enable you to access being present and in the present, but also to start to work on the first of three fundamental parts that I believe open the doorway wide open to happiness.

Connection is one of the most important and powerful things on this planet, and possibly even in the universe.

It is as integral to our existence as water, food and shelter. It is everything from hate to love.

The way you feel when you see a mesmerising sunset for instance is just one of the connections to that event that you will have created. You will have a million memories from your senses attached to that experience. You will know stories and have seen sunsets before that connect this experience to then, and you can recall and make comparisons. You are a hub of connection. If you can perceive it, you are connected to it.

All of the wonderful and terrible things that this world has seen has been the result of a powerful connection. Different perspectives and understandings of the world have encouraged such motivation as all of the wars the world has hosted and unfortunately, will continue to host, and all of the beautiful moments of selflessness, bravery and the wholehearted mission to create a better way of living through equality, love and respect for all.

I believe the way to creating your own happiness is creating a life where the connections in your life are congruent, positive and enriching, and where those which are incongruent, negative and draining are rare or even absent.

The three areas of connection that, if engaged with congruently and continually, will result in a boost of instant and sustained, long-term happiness are:

- **Connection with Self:** That is, knowing who you are, how you are, and what you like and dislike.

- **Connection with the Environment:** The physical place (and the emotional connections that you currently have and that are created in that place).

- **Connection with Others:** Your engagement

with other human beings and whether those people think, feel and behave in a way that is congruent with who and how you are.

Connection to self is debatably the most important area because it impacts the others profoundly. In truth, they are all interconnected, but the others are dependent on you knowing yourself.

This doesn't mean you have to take a two-week tribal trek to northern Mexico, spend time with the Huichol and eat peyote on a journey of personal discovery. What it means is that you can begin engaging with all three areas, and the better you know yourself, the further you can progress with the other two.

Connection with yourself is really rather simple when it comes down to it. It is essentially listening to that feeling inside you when you ask, "Do I really want to do this?"

For some people giving away their first crisp from a fresh packet is akin to worshipping the Devil, a big no no. And for others it's not a problem at all.

If you are one of those who feels the urge inside to pretend you haven't opened the packet yet because you don't want to give your first crisp away, congruence for you would be not sharing it and agreeing with that inner feeling, and that would make you happy, you evil, evil person.

Incongruence for you would be giving the first crisp anyway and feeling that yucky feeling inside as well as the somewhat superficial happiness associated with being selfless.

Before I move on from here, I would like to add this. Who you are right now, today, isn't who you will always be. As an example, with practise and a good connection to the reason(s) why you're going to do it; you could actually learn to love being the person who gives their first crisp away. I used to be that, "It's my crisp!" person. I would always spy the best roast potatoes at dinner time and sneak them for myself. Now, I enjoy not taking those even if it is simply to feel that freedom from attachment. I don't need it and because I want it, I let someone else enjoy it. Sometimes.

Connection with your environment is again, rather simple. It is being in a place where your surroundings make you feel happy. That means, if you hate being indoors and surrounded by grey walls and laminate furniture; and you love getting muddy and being around wildlife; to be congruent to who you are would be to NOT work in an office and create a way for you do what you want to do in an environment better suited to your personality. That isn't to say if you are doing your dream job, but it involves you being in an office, that you should pack up and move to the Amazon rainforest. It means create a way for you to love your environment. Even if that means at the very least, if you hate being in the city but right now in your dream job that's where you must be, then love where you are simply for facilitating you to be doing what you love. And if you really can't do that, then make a change. Loving where you are is important in being happy. Where you are might not be amazing, but making that positive connection could change everything for you.

Connection to others is a little more tricky. In order to really connect with others, you need to know who you are, and then connect with them from that place. Coming from a place of what you think they expect or what you expect they expect of you is just one messy way of building very poor and surface-level relationships.

Humans thrive from having relationships, we are social creatures and when things don't go right, we find it very easy to get hurt. And then we change, and then we build shallow relationships so that we don't get hurt and become vulnerable, and then we wonder why those relationships too deteriorate and/or feel superficial and weak.

Truly connecting with others involves going skin deep, and that's scary, because to do that you need to allow yourself to become vulnerable. In doing so, you open up an opportunity to get hurt at the very same time that you create that opportunity to feel something amazing.

What we are going to do now is create a list of you. This is of what you love, what you don't love, what makes you feel great, what makes you feel like crap. What you love doing and what you don't love doing. What I want you to do is on a piece of paper, draw a line down the middle and on the left-hand side write:

"People, places, habits and things that FILL me with energy."

And on the right-hand side:

"People, places, habits and things that DRAIN me of energy."

Use colour pens, give it detail, the more of yourself you give to this the more you will gain. One word answers will give you equally vague direction. Once you have a full and comprehensive list on either side, carry on reading.

I know that this is exciting and you want to get to the next bit, but imagine right now that the next bit didn't exist, and all you had was this one exercise. Give it your all!

What you now have in front of you should be a lovingly

embellished piece of paper. What you also have is a very telling document.

The first thing you might realise now is just how much you actually know about yourself. Did you really know 100% that some of those things drained/filled you with energy?

The second thing is that the things you listed on the left-hand side that fill you with energy are most certainly also things that you love.

The third thing, and the one that may surprise you the most, is how full your left-hand column is, and how little of it you actually engage with regularly. You may also notice how much of your life is actually spent in the right-hand side of your paper.

There may be some things that will show up in both columns for you. This is normal! I have seen many panicked faces from people who think they must be the only person to have this happen to them, before trying to come to terms with the fact that they are uniquely screwed. Do not worry!

The document you have just created is your action plan. By your own hand, if you could live in the left-hand (interestingly the creative side of the brain) side of your page, you would live a happy life full of the people, places, habits and things that not only fill you with energy, but also that you love.

Experiment 3:

Your experiment is to begin using this new document as your action plan to life.

You will start transitioning your world from the right to the left hand side of the page.

Question 22: *Which items on the right-hand side of the page can you immediately cut out?*

Question 23: *Which items can you edit or change to make energising?*

Some of your items in the right-hand column may only be there because they are something you feel you 'should' or you 'have to' engage with because you have no choice.

Question 24: *Knowing that you choose to engage with all of the things that drain you that you believe you 'have to' and 'need to' engage with; what do you want to do about them, and how do you want to feel about them?*

As you continue through this book and even after that, use this document that you have created as a personal guide. Keep updating it, keep editing it (it feels amazing to draw a line through right-hand items!)

Question 25: *In what ways specifically could your life be more amazing if you lived more in the left-hand side of your page?*

You know you are the only one who can make that happen, if you choose to.

Fig 7: Draw you as a connector, connecting to all of the amazing, energising things you want in your life.

Feel Free To Say Anything
(Just don't necessarily say anything freely)

In keeping with the idea of connection, and chiefly, knowing oneself, I have an exercise that has in many cases been pivotal in the journey of self-discovery, self-acceptance, and has been a supportive bridge for the transition from living a closed-off and somewhat disconnected life, to living a more congruent, free and open life, which will make you happier.

There is a stipulation to this happiness however that I want to address.

While being you, doing you and becoming congruent with who you really are is certainly a direct pathway to living a happy and fulfilled life, there are some ways in which it may at points create situations that might not make you so happy.

No matter what point in your life you are at, you will have lived in a certain way. Those ways will have been what you have communicated to those around you via your interactions, and as a result, those around you will have connected with you as that person.

If you begin to embrace areas of yourself that you haven't otherwise been communicating with, the current relationships you have will be affected. This could be positively – providing those involved are prepared to accept you for who you are – and positively if they are not prepared to accept you for who you are and change the way they behave towards you and/or leave.

You'll notice I said positively twice. Whether negativity actually exists when it comes to labelling a circumstance or action you are involved with is debatable. After all you have no idea what doors will open up to you following that *'negative'* experience. For all you know, (which like everyone else is something between nothing and next to nothing regarding the future) that 'negative' experience could have resulted in the greatest things in your life yet to come, therefore making it a truly monumental positive experience.

In the case of you connecting more with yourself, if you become who you really are and are congruent with yourself you will, as a result, feel more deeply and wholeheartedly happy. Again, this happiness might be in the moments in which you are acting in congruence, this might be all of the time. You should also not ignore wider factors and other areas that you believe could make you unhappy such as biological factors for instance.

From this place you have a great base and foundation to build the wonderful empire that is your life.

Question 26: *If as a result of you being congruent others are not happy. What does that mean to you?*

Question 27: *If as a result you being congruent others are not happy. What might it mean about them? (give more than one answer)*

Question 28: *To what extent would your world end if those who were unhappy with you being congruent weren't in your life?*

Question 29: *What could you do to help those who are unhappy with you being congruent to see how you now see?*

Choosing to be happy then, really is a life decision.

In order to bridge the gap between deciding to be happy and congruent, and communicating every second of that to everyone around you (which could induce some kind of shock) you may benefit from exploring your answers to these questions, and take down some of the first and most difficult walls in beginning this process.

In addition to this, from now until you feel comfortable enough with who you are and also comfortable enough to fully be yourself 100% of the time you are going to write a daily diary. In it, you are going to be completely open, and completely vulnerable.

Each day you will add a new entry. It may be, "I had a curious dream about Zach Efron." If for you that is something very personal. I want you to consider this special diary as your ultimate confidént. Tell it stuff you wouldn't tell your partner or your friends. Tell it stuff you barely want to know about yourself. And then, and here is where you make the difference. Accept those things. You would be doing yourself a great disservice in writing down these things and judging and analysing yourself. This is a judgement free zone. The only person to hurt you or make you feel bad here truly and clearly is you. What you write doesn't mean you are a *'bad'* person or a *'good'* person. You are just a person, writing things.

Que Sera, Sera
(No, really)

You may well be familiar with the very famous song by Doris Day. You may have even tried in brief to live by that idealistic lifestyle and failed because well, let's face it, what will be is usually going to be s***.

Except, it really doesn't have to be. I prefer to think of life as, "What is, is." Honestly, how much more do we need to frighten ourselves by thinking of the mysterious and unknown things we are going to have to deal with in the future? No, let's bring it all back to now, the present.

What is, is. Has there ever been anything truer? What is, is. Now there is a reason and an explanation for everything. There are causes and factors involved with every 'good' and 'bad' thing on this planet. But none of those matter, really, when the cold, hard, bottom-line is that whatever is happening, is happening. And as soon as it is done happening, within a millionth of a second it is in the irreparable past and it is then something that has happened. The things you do, think and feel; and have done, thought and felt are what they are. And you have felt them. Now you can spend hours and days and years of your life ruminating and worrying and getting annoyed and placing blame and feeling emotional and hurt and numerous other exhausting things. But none of that really matters. However long you decide you need to hurt and hold onto something will not change what has happened.

Question 30: *What would your life be like if you put all of your 'flaws' and problems, and areas where you are wonderful, and areas where you are a terrible human being, all out into the light and you just said:*

"This is me. I don't have to like it, in fact I don't and there are some things now that I can clearly see in this light that I want to change. But right now this is me. And that is okay."

To say, "Right now this is the result of everything I have seen, done and felt and there is no need to go deep into my memories and psychoanalyse myself. I know that what is, is. And that is okay. I do not want to cut bits out that I don't like, because then I won't be whole. All of this is me. I do not hate anything about myself, even the *'horrible'* bits. They happened because they happened. And they are what they are. And today, that is okay. What is, is. And I have the power to grow and develop and change. I am okay."

Acceptance is a powerful thing, and it takes yourself to look at yourself and say, "I know I am not everything I want to be, nor have I always done what I now perceive to have been the best. But I am human. Today is a new day. And I am okay."

Once you have truly accepted who you are, it opens up the door for others to accept you too. And more than this, it gives them a blessing and permission for them to accept themselves and that is an incredible gift. You could even try and palm it off at Christmas time if you're that way inclined!

It can be humbling to remember that none of us are more than human. We all do stupid things. We all do things often we wished we hadn't (though actually if you hadn't you wouldn't know now what you now know). It is okay.

I know that this might sound like nonsense to you. Why would you believe this? You have lived your entire life in a different way and now, at whatever age you are there is a solution? Forget it. You want to defend your defective way of being, because it's your way. And that's okay. You will do what you do, and right now, whatever you choose is what you believe is best for you. Even if your interests are to make sure you don't get hurt or embarrassed or feel afraid of what it might take to engage with this. Before we continue, I have an experiment for you.

Experiment 4:

Re-read the speech again starting with, "This is me. I don't have to like it..." and ending, "And I have the power to grow and develop and change. I am okay.'"

You can change the words to make it more personal. This is about you. And If right now you want to keep that word for word, that too is alright. Read it and re-read it until you feel 'AS IF' you are closer to accepting yourself. If that moment comes soon, keep reading it and notice how the way you think and feel about yourself changes.

In addition to your daily diary commitments, read that passage to yourself each morning. Remember also your commitment to the conditions of this book. Believe it until proven wrong. Act 'AS IF' it were true and give it the best chance by fully engaging. This is your life, and it is your life you won't be making how you want by letting any fear or reservation keep you from engaging with an open mind.

Fig 8: Draw what it feels like to you to accept yourself.

Taking The Ultimate Chill Pill
(3,2,1, mellow)

Don't do drugs kids! Adults however... I jest. This is far from an exciting receipt of permission to go and get high. Though when practised, taking this fully will result in a boost of calm and happiness.

How often do you find yourself annoyed at something or someone else? "It's stupid", "It doesn't make sense", "They're just so argumentative and stubborn."

Sound at all familiar? It may do because that is that kind of bull crap we have to deal with each and every day. What about waiting in a really long line in a supermarket? Worse still, what about swapping lines and the one you were originally in goes faster? Can you feel your heart racing already?

We secretly love to get stressed. It's an exciting injection of drama into our lives and an easy way of venting about stuff we have no control over.

Except those things we believe we have no control over, we often actually do. Nothing and nobody can make you feel anything. Nobody possesses so much power over you. They can do or be or say things and as a result of that stimulus you respond in a certain way, but you chose that way. As a result of culture, conditioning, whatever it is for you, you are getting annoyed and feel unhappy when you could equally be happy in that exact situation.

As well as accepting yourself (flaws and all); to really create happiness in your own life, you would benefit from accepting others (flaws and all). Again, you do not have to like what they do and who they are, you do not have to even understand it. Simply, by accepting it as something that is, you can subtract a huge chunk of unhappiness from your life.

This isn't the whole story to taking a chill pill however, because people will do things that you don't understand, that you know 100% indisputably are wrong. It may affect your life, but remember also they are living theirs, and it probably affects theirs more.

So if somebody is going to do something you know is going to go wrong, and you've told them and there's nothing else you can actually do to change their intentions. That's okay. Accept it as what is and do the best that you can to make sure that it harms or damages you and others as little as possible. And when it does go the way you knew it would all along, accept also that everyone in some way has benefited from that happening, even if you or they don't know quite how right now.

If someone is trying their best and it's still not good enough for you. Assess the importance of what the 'good enough' is for. If it really doesn't matter. Accept it. Accept them for being the best that they can be. And if you can do that, try loving them for it.

If someone is being a complete arsehole and you don't want to deal with them anymore. You could get angry and upset or you could just accept it as a fact. "They are an arsehole and something very major in their life isn't right. I hope they're okay. I can accept that what is, is, and move on from today by making a difference in my life."

I appreciate that this idea of acceptance sounds so magical, almost as if in writing this I had slipped away to join the fairies and gnomes that reside in my garden. Perhaps even your commitments to the Conditions are being challenged here.

I want to reassure you and remind you that this is not a case of, "This is fact, now believe it." It is a case of, this is an important experiment that you are going to take part in to see how amazing your life can become as a result, and how truly happy you can be.

Experiment 5:

Test this idea of acceptance out, experience situations where you feel unhappy with external factors and accept them. Make notes on what happens (even better, add these to your daily diary.) Record how you respond, how they respond, what you notice was different to your expectations, what you notice was similar to your expectations. Notice also the simple fact that you had expectations which could also influence your experience.

You will fail miserably the first time, and the second, and perhaps even all the way to the hundredth. This is, as with everything else in life, about practise and engagement. Give it your all, repeat it and repeat it and notice it get easier. Notice how your mind and body responds differently as the experiment goes on. And as the experiment goes on, up the stakes, accept truly terrible people. Become a master of acceptance. This is your life. This is your game. This is your opportunity to truly be happy. You have only yourself to stop you.

Part of your journey to acceptance and indeed vulnerability is experiencing vulnerability and acceptance from and in others.

I want to share something personal with you.

I was once in a relationship, shocking I know, and we had a very abrupt, very fast break-up. I wasn't quite sure exactly why she had chosen to split, and for a little while that bothered me, almost as if in knowing the reasons I could somehow fix it. And after I realised it wasn't going to get fixed, it then bothered me because I felt like I needed that closure. To know why it happened so that I could lay it to rest, like a detective in a horror movie clearing down a crime scene so that the spirit of the ghost that had been haunting the lovely new family from the city could be put to rest.

After I realised I was never going to 'know' why exactly what happened did so, I realised also that the best way for me to move on was to do just that. I'd spent so long living in the past of trying to understand it all, that I hadn't given any thought to living in this moment.

I chose to accept what happened. It was what it was, even though I didn't know why.

I chose to accept myself for everything that I had and hadn't done. For all of the things I knew as a result of the break-up that I could have done differently to make us both feel better while in the relationship.

And I chose to accept her, though this perplexed some of those with whom I spoke afterwards. I wanted to accept her because she did what she felt was best. Because she, as every single one of us does, has her right to freewill. I don't have to like what happened, or how it happened. But the only difference I can make to that situation today is how I feel and act and respond to it, today. I choose to accept it. Because the alternative would be to ruminate and spend time, energy and effort feeling unhappy about an event that no longer exists.

With every single second life continues. With every single second you have a fresh start and a choice.

Question 31: *Every single second I have a fresh start and a choice. How do I choose to feel right now?*

Question 32: *Every single second I have a fresh start and a choice. How do I choose to live right now?*

Question 33: *Every single second I have a fresh start and a choice. Who, in this second, do I choose to be?*

Answer these questions with candour. Once you have your answers. Commit to them. Each and every one. If you commit to living your life in that way, in this second, you can be certain that when your future comes, you will be living it in that way. When you are in the present and living in line with these commitments, the legacy of the way you chose to live your future through your actions in the present will reflect that.

I appreciate that while the idea of being able to just 'turn on' acceptance to things that might bother you may be difficult to get your head around, actually acting on it may seem impossible to you; after all, you've lived your entire life in a very different way. You've grown up being conditioned to hold onto situations and fight for your feelings until something gives and breaks. I want to provide some stepping stones to this magical place of open acceptance.

Earlier in this chapter, I touched on how no one has the power to control how you feel. It's all you. So when someone does something that stirs emotions in you, what you are feeling is *your* emotional response, developed from years of experiences, to the stimulus they are providing.

This is the first stepping stone. Remember, they have only done something. Without your interpretation, what they have done is neither good nor bad. This means that really, you can't be angry or upset at them for how you feel. You may not actually be angry or upset at what they have done at all, and that therefore that may make it easy to accept. Instead, you may be feeling things because of what their actions *meant* to you. This is where acceptance gets difficult.

No matter how accepting you are of what physically happened, your emotions, which are personally influenced and therefore often unreliable as a form of evidence, are more hardy and may require special treatment to reach a *'happy place'*. Here is the second stepping stone.

Remembering that what you are feeling is personal, self-created, and not the fault of someone or something else. You may choose to take action to help you in resolving your own emotions. This action is a calculated and specific action and it comes with some guidelines.

Firstly, it should not harm others in any way. Full stop. Secondly, it should be process specific, not outcome specific. The reason why this action is process specific is because you can't really control an outcome. If you based an action, that you believed would help you personally resolve your emotional responses to a situation, upon an outcome specific goal, if you didn't get that exact outcome, you could be chasing your tail and wasting your time/life/energy/effort for a long time. Being process orientated means that you know, once you have done what you are planning on doing, simply by doing it, you have resolved your own emotions.

The third guideline for this action towards acceptance is that you hold yourself accountable. This basically means you don't make your process specific action to confront someone and tell them that what they have done has upset you. Rather, because of your own life experiences, you got upset at what has happened.

As you read this, what you may find is that you actually don't want to take action at all, because you realise the situation isn't really about them. It's about you. You may also not want to take action because you realise that in doing so, you will be projecting your own emotional map onto them, and in some ways, that just doesn't make sense, does it?

It's Nothing Personal
(No, really, it's not)

Listen, I know you're special, you truly are. And you are a handsome devil, but, and I'm sorry to break it to you, to most people, you're not actually that important.

"Really", I hear you gasp. But bear with me, because actually you're probably less important than you may have even imagined… in a good way.

Part of being able to accept and actually be okay with some of the things we think are horrible and make us unhappy is understanding more about them. That's not to say if a guy tries to chop your arm off you should sit with him, make him a tea and ask him to reveal all about his logic. But, appreciating a different perspective can certainly make you happier.

You, like me, like everyone else on this planet have your own *'stuff'* going on. Your boss for instance may have been having an affair and this morning was caught out. Your partner may have used your toothbrush this morning only to discover that in a drunken moment of inspiration the night before, you decided to clean between your toes with it and now you're not on talking terms. Anything and everything happens to us in our own lives. And we are human, it's hard to keep it in, it's hard to speak it out. It's hard not to let the things that happen to us as our lives inevitably move on, minute by minute, affect the way we consequentially feel and behave.

The fact is, you have no idea of what is going on in someone else's life. And even if you think you might, you have no idea how they are experiencing it because the way that they are experiencing their life is informed by every event they have ever lived. Even if they were to sit with you and explain many of their life events to add context, the thing that's currently going on with them wouldn't have changed and affected you in the same ways that it is changing and is affecting them. This also explains why something that might seem insignificant to some people, for example, getting a scratch on your red car, could send you loopy. They have no idea that once upon a time when you were young and had little money you dreamed of having a red car to love and behold. Our present is very much informed by how we have experienced and interpreted and continue to interpret our past.

So, where this brings you today is here. Nothing is personal. Nothing is about you. The person in the office who is always having a go at you? Yep, they're dealing with their sexually challenging feelings for you. The woman who is trying to throw a brick through your car window? She broke a nail today and has decided that nothing in her world can go right. You, my friend, are just caught in the crossfire. Deal with it. Accept it.

And don't for one second take it personally and feel it; unless you want to be unhappy and stressed and full of drama, in which case knock yourself out.

Experiment 6:

Nothing is personal. When you find yourself in situations where you start to feel upset, offended, victimised or unhappy because of something that someone is doing at/toward you remember, nothing is personal.

This is a tough one and involves a lot of ignoring your well-trained mind that will be shouting, "They're being mean to you!" And deciding despite this that you know it is not about you.

Remember, this is not about blind belief, this is about testing a theory.

"If I believe, wholeheartedly with complete committed conviction that what is happening to me that is making me unhappy, whatever it may be, is not truly and 100% a personal and unique experience and about me, I will become happier."

And the only way to discover your answer to this hypothesis is to agree with it, test it and find out. This involves as you know, believing until proven correct/incorrect and repeating the test in a variety of different situations.

Worrying About Future Events That Haven't Happened And Might Not Ever Happen?

It sounds ridiculous, doesn't it. Worrying about future, (and therefore imagined events), that haven't happened and might not ever happen.

A defence I'm sure you have probably come across for this is, "I'm just planning in case it does happen", "I'm just being prepared", "I'm preparing myself."

Oh, well in that case have you purchased your ninja suit for when Bill and Ted return and zap you back to the Ming dynasty to train you up to become the world's most prolific ninja? No, why not? That too is something that is a potential made-up future.

Alright, so usually, the things you're worrying about are a little more *'realistic'* than that, but only really because those stories use people and things that you know exist.

In fact, all worry is based in the future. You can't worry about the past, that's already happened. You can't worry about the present because it's already gone. You're worrying about an event that doesn't yet exist, and so can be created or not created, and if it is created, most certainly won't play out the way you have imagined and replayed it in your mind. How often does anything ever meet an expectation dead on?

Worryingly, worrying is a very powerful form of a self-fulfilling prophecy. The more you worry about a certain thing happening, the more your behaviour will facilitate that exact thing to happen. And when it does happen you'll only have yourself to blame while wondering why your life is so awful and why you can always see the *'bad'* things happening before they do and not the *'good'*.

Perhaps that is simply because you don't expect the *'good'*.

How often do you find yourself thinking so intently about creating a positive outcome that your behaviour facilitates that good thing to come to fruition? Exactly. Fruit for thought perhaps.

Someone very close to me has developed a penchant for anxiety. They do it very well and regularly. I'm not sure how much you understand about the idea of neuroplasticity, but it demonstrates that for as long as you are alive, your actions alter the way that your brain functions. As you do your life, your brain creates bridges between certain areas of itself and you develop skills and behaviours to make those things that you do, better, smoother, and more habitual.

So, if you do anxiety, you'll get better at it, and it'll be increasingly easier to access and increasingly more difficult to change. But certainly not impossible.

She asked me for ways and techniques to stop being anxious. We began with STOP therapy. This is where you create in your mind a big, loud, bright, bold STOP sign. Put it in neon lights and paint it glow in the dark. Give it some fog siren sounds and whenever you get even the slightest thought of anxious worry. STOP! After that if you try to go back to that thought, STOP! You know that you are smart and you are putting that sign there in your mind for a reason, so STOP and continue to STOP until you get sick of tired of hearing that awful sound in your head and seeing that sign because you're concerned you might soon develop epilepsy.

This worked to a degree, but it required dedication, focus and attention for an indefinite period of time, which can be tiresome. I wondered if there was something deeper. Something more potent with which to spike the root of this way of living. There was.

Humans are instinctively programmed for preservation. We do not want to die. We do not want to feel pain because that leads to dying and that therefore feels like what we imagine dying to be like. We are often risk averse and do not challenge social norms because if we challenge that norm, we may be alone. And if we are alone we do not have the tribe to survive with, to feed us and give us the social interaction we gravely desire.

This inhibits innovation. It inhibits a great deal in fact. And it also means that people are constantly worried about what others think, and the potential consequences of their actions on their imagined future.

At the core of worry, which is essentially a behaviour of anxiety, is loss.

There is no worry without the fear of losing something.

If you are worrying about something, which will be making you unhappy, engage with this interrogative exercise:

Question 34: *I am worried about (state your worry.) I am fearful that this worry will come true because it will damage/ hurt/ kill/ I will lose/ I will not gain (state the things you are afraid of losing as a result of this worry's manifestation.) This worries me because (what that means to you.)*

Now ask yourself what that means, and then what that means and continue to do this until you know the very soul of this worry. Usually in seeing it, it evaporates along with the fear of losing whatever it was you were afraid of losing.

I want to share an example with you because it can be very easy to get lost in unspecific stories:

A teacher mentions to another that one of their colleagues demonstrated something to the class in a way that he wouldn't have. No judgement of that demonstration was passed and the conversation ends neutrally there. They both go home and get on with their lives. The teacher who made the comment however is now worrying. He is concerned that his colleague will tell the teacher he was talking about what he said, or tell their managers and there will be negative consequences. He desperately wants to call up the person with whom he spoke to say, "Don't say anything" but that might be weird, or it might even make them think more about it and feel that they should say something. So now this teacher is at home, sitting quietly feeling as if he is going crazy. He also feels as if he is unable to communicate what he is thinking because he knows it is crazy and irrational, but somehow it is rational enough to be a real reality for him.

Question 35: *What do I fear losing as a result of this imaginary scenario/set of scenarios coming true?*

Would be a great place for this teacher to begin resolving their concerns.

The answers could be endless. Depending on who this person is they could vary wildly. He could fear:

- Losing friends
- Losing trust in the workplace

- Losing integrity of his word
- Being told off and feeling belittled and like a child
- Feeling socially outcast
- Feeling untrusted
- Thinking people think of him in a way that he is not
- Losing his job
- Losing the comfortable feeling environment at work that he currently enjoys

The list goes on. And in fact if you created a list of the possible outcomes to his situation as a result of his actions, the actual event would probably fall somewhere between the best-case scenario of; nothing negative happens and the person that he was talking about brings in cake the next day. And the worst-case scenario where he gets fired for being an awful backstabbing human being and being the only person to cause any degree of workplace drama in the company, and then he dies.

The truly insane thing here is that nothing has actually happened. At least nothing to be perceived by any person of sound body and mind that could be seen as negative. And yet the feelings of worry have brought to the present the imaginary feelings attached to that made-up event, as if the imagined situations had actually happened.

So regardless of whether or not the things actually will happen, the feelings associated with those things happening are already a reality.

If for example you imagine you are being judged without proof of this, you will feel judged whether or not it is true.

In worrying about whatever it is that you are worrying about, you have imagined or dreamt up a terrible idea (daymare) and have decided that for whatever reason such as an inventive and punishing way to prepare yourself for the future, that you will actually LIVE that daymare right now. As in right now in this second, the only second you ever have to choose if you want to be happy or unhappy.

Question 36: *What if you just knew that you did what you did, and that you are smart enough to be able to deal with anything that may happen in the future? What would be different?*

After all, you've done that so far and you are still alive.

Question 37: *How could life be then for you?*

Question 38: *How would you feel and think differently about any given situation if you functioned from that place?*

I understand that trying to 'logic' your way out of anxiety does not always, or even frequently provide close to 100% clear-minded resolution.

The truth is, you know all of this. Sometimes a reminder helps, but other times you just know and feel as if you still can't get over your desire to choose to worry.

For now, answer these questions as best you can and discover some new, deeper answers to know yourself better. In the coming chapters, you will get the tools to fully dispose of this parasite. Great work so far! Keep it up!

Thinking Life Into Existence

We've just covered a great deal to do with thinking negatively and worrying, and to add to that I would like to share an interesting perspective. One that you are going to experiment with and one which is true for you, until proven completely incorrect under your agreement with reading this book.

Everything in your world is unique to you. The way you see, hear, feel and understand the world may just be solely yours, if even in a very small way.

You therefore create your own reality. Your reality happens as a result of the choices you make, and the actions you take and that is all based on how you read your world.

Question 39: *What if by imagining all of the 'terrible' ways your life could end up, what if by simply entertaining those ideas as possibilities, you are in some way facilitating those existences into a potential reality of yours?*

Question 40: *What if by imagining that horrible outcome as a possibility, it actually becomes a* *possibility that you worry about, and then your actions start to direct you towards that as a result of your focus and attention?*

It's very possible. As we addressed earlier, according to quantum physics, anything is possible. In the realms of all of the things that appear to be impossible, this ranks far, far down at the bottom, wouldn't you agree?

It's not unheard of, people's lives going the way their minds lean. In fact that is often the advice many *'successful'* people boast, "Think as if you are successful, not going to be, you are. Make it real and focus on it, and it'll happen." Heck, is that not what things like, *'The Law Of Attraction'* is all about? It's big stuff.

However, living such a terrible life might be exactly what you want. There may be many benefits of living such a life.

One of our greatest fears is failure. As illogical as it sounds, for many people, choosing to fail is a safer feeling place than trying and failing (it saves the ego a lot of trouble). They can die knowing they never realised they weren't capable. Or were.

Living that nightmare reality might just be the perfect hiding place for you. A safe place where you don't have to face the reality where you are in control. Where you actually have the power to make a difference. At least in this hiding place you can blame, *'The Man'*.

Experiment 7:

What I am asking you to do here is be very honest, and ask yourself what those not-so-great alternative realities you have created for yourself are. Before you dispatch them, write them down in as much detail as you believe you possibly can and one by one go through them asking yourself throughout: "How does this benefit me?"

Again, this is not a trick question. You are a smart and intelligent human being. You don't do anything, ever, unless it benefits you. Even briefly imagining the idea of these awful realities without fully creating them will have benefited you in some way.

Once you have answers to every single scenario. Ask yourself this:

Question 41: *In what ways is this/ are these benefit(s) derived from fear?*

They will be.

The next step is all you. You have all the information you require to make the next most beneficial decision in your life.

Question 42: *Am I going to choose to act out of fear and preservation? Am I going to admit and be accountable to myself that I am owned by my fears and sitting frightened in the passenger seat?*

Or;

Question 43: *Am I going to decide to take action against living those realities, and for a new more empowering one. To sit at the wheel and own everything that is me, including my fears?*

As this book is a guide to happiness, I can tell you that while you will feel moments of numb bliss in coming from a place of fear and preservation, there is a great deal more happiness to be created in the world of accountability and abundance.

Having lived in both worlds, I can tell you that there really is no looking back once you decide to take full ownership of your life. Not because you can't, but because living that way just doesn't make sense to do anymore.

The experiment I pose to you is to dispose of your unwanted realities, stop any new ones as you feel you're beginning to create them and answer a loud, "No!" to question 42, and a powerful, bold and confident "Ohhhh Yeahhhh!" To question 43.

Fig 9: Draw a representation of you choosing happiness.

Today Is A Good Day To Die

Three cheers for morbidity! Hip hip, hurray! Hip hip, hurray! Hip hip, hurray!

In a book designed to act as a guide on how to create happiness in your life, it might seem a bit out of place to again be speaking of death, let alone designating an entire chapter to it!

But death is incredibly important to life, in fact, without death, life would simply come to a complete and rapid stop… and then everything would die.

That salad you're eating there, dead lettuce. That fly you see over there, yep, it's eating your dead skin particles.

Life on a daily basis performs in a beautiful ballet with death, and yet we have found so many ways to use it as a reason and an excuse to stop our own lives from being as amazing and fulfilled as possible.

As children we are warned about our mortality. In the moments where we had the most fun, most of us were doing something hazardous to our health. Our guardians would undoubtedly call, "Take care" and "Be safe" which essentially meant, "Don't take risks or have fun because I don't want to have to take you to the hospital."

Death, as explained in a previous chapter is also the reason why you choose to suffer. Because you are afraid of something ending, dying, going away, and that can really put a strangle-hold on things.

The emotional attachment you have built with all of the things in your life is quite literally weighing you down and grounding you, because God forbid you lose those things!

The fact is however, death is natural. Things need to end. If nothing ended, nothing could begin. If your life as a baby didn't end, you'd never have know the joys of puberty, and if that didn't die, you'd never have known the joys of a consistent vocal pattern and facial hair that is coarse and pube-like.

The most demanding area of death to deal with, that we dice with everyday, is our metaphorical deaths. Thankfully most of us right now are not in a position to worry about our literal mortality, but I will take this moment to remind you that actually, many people living in every single country around the world, including this one are in that position.

In everyday life you side-step congruence because being congruent could result in saying or doing something that others don't like or agree with, and *that* could harm your ego. And well, if your ego is hurt, that hurts you personally doesn't it? And then, if those people feel that way towards you, perhaps you'll be excluded from the tribe and die alone. You don't want to do that. It's better to preserve your life by acting incongruently and being more unhappy.

You have symbols and talismans scattered around you that you call *'stuff'* that you have an emotional attachment to, and everything has a meaning. Your new expensive mobile phone means to tell us that you are doing well in life, and you want others to know.

The book your parent gave to you just before you left home is important because it reminds you of that time. You don't actually read it, but you have it as a reminder. It would be terrible if that were to go, wouldn't it?

This is what I mean by being afraid of death. You are, as everyone in the world is too, afraid to lose things because those things mean something to you. To lose those would mean that they have, metaphorically at least, died, because they have ended in your life and have gone away.

Your experience and understanding of this kind of death may differ greatly from how you feel about being afraid of actually dying. Curiously, more people are comfortable with this than dying to things within life, i.e. breaking their connection/attachment to specific things, people and ideas etc, even though without being alive, they couldn't have those things.

When you come from this place of being afraid of death, you are also coming from a place of preservation. That is, keeping something and locking down the doors so it can't leave.

The reason why this can result in unhappiness is because for a start, it is exhausting living in lockdown. It is a world full of worry and very few new footsteps in new directions, lest you leave the things and life you are trying to hold onto for fear they become vulnerable.

You are also coming from a place of poverty. In feeling you need to preserve something, you on some level believe that it is rare and fleeting. The reason you keep the book isn't because you're going to read it again because you love reading it, it's because you worry that if you got rid of it, it would mean something about how you feel towards your parents or that experience. You worry that you would forget (and the memory would fade i.e. become rare and fleeting) and that moment you hold close and that is important to you will become more distant and further from you.

What happens when you are in a lockdown situation? What happens when you hold onto something with both hands?

True, whatever you are preserving will better be preserved. But with two hands occupied, all of the similar, superlative experiences yet to come will go un-captured and will be unable to get in. You are putting a cap on the level of feeling you want to feel, in case the feeling before goes and you won't be able to replace it.

Learning to die doesn't mean clearing out your house and becoming numb to the world, it means being okay with things coming and going. You embrace abundance, you embrace change and all of a sudden the risks you perceived to be attached to the potential changes you have dreamed of making in your life, to live a life closer to that which you have dreamed, become less threatening. The things you wanted to access that you believed would lead to a happier life aren't so far away. And the reasons you so abundantly provided yourself to not do certain things, the worries, the fears, the limitations don't make sense. When you're not afraid to lose, then all you have is gain. You learn from your experiences either way, the worst-case scenario is that your situation changes and it is not what you wanted. You are still living. The best-case scenario is that you begin living more of your ideal life, in which case you really will be living.

Experiment 8:

Your newest experiment is to practise dying. End things in your life that are no longer serving you that you have held onto because of fear. Fears like, you don't know what would happen if you did. You're scared you won't find something like that again (is that a bad thing if it's not working?) Things that you have used as a crutch and an excuse to keep you from not taking action in your life. Or simply things you keep for sentiment.

It is not an easy thing to do. When what you are dying to is so deeply connected to you, it feels as if you actually might die. But the feeling afterwards, when you release that attachment to something, that weight is released and I kid you not, you'll feel lighter.

All of a sudden life doesn't seem so serious. If something comes then that's great. If it goes, that's okay too, it just means more of that wonderful thing can come.

Here are some lyrics that really resonate with this idea:

"It's been too hard living, but I'm afraid to die.
Because I don't know what's up there,
beyond the sky.

It's been a long, long time coming but I know,
change gonna come."

Change Gonna Come – Sam Cooke

That's Hardly Realistic Now, Is It?
(The confused land of expectation)

Well, what did you expect? This book would be light on its feet and nice and shallow? I told you, I'm not into all of that superficial stuff.

And now that we've covered death, let's dive face first into another deep way in which we make ourselves unhappy, and then explore how in knowing that, you can create your own happiness this very second.

A great deal of unhappiness boils down to loss. But, closely linked and just as impactful as loss we have it's deadly twin, lack.

Lack lives in the land of expectancy. You see, if something genuinely lacks something, it just lacks it. There is no emotional result there. However, when a human being with emotions comes onto the scene, that's when it all gets hairy.

Imagine you have a brand new go kart. You want to build it and take it out for a spin. You do build most of it and realise that you lack the important nuts to make it usable. Now in this situation, you simply don't have them. But you know at some point you can go and get them. However that doesn't matter. You now have a wonderful opportunity to be unhappy.

And oh are you going to take advantage of that! You can get upset at not having them, you can get annoyed at yourself for not getting them and you can get annoyed at someone else for their role in this all too.

Besides all of this being highly unproductive and doing absolutely nothing to give remedy to the situation where you simply need nuts, besides the fact that you have chosen to indulge in the very egocentric experience of unhappy wallowing. You are doing this because of yourself. If you hadn't expected to be zipping around that day, in that moment, it wouldn't have bothered you at all. But now that you believe that you could have been, (in the same way that you could have ridden a lion to the supermarkets in the imaginary future) you have an opportunity to feel unhappy.

You feel that the lack of meeting your desired expectancy has resulted in the loss of your desired experience. And that is truly terrible.

Lack can also plague you in an even more invasive way. Say, "Hello" to the dreaded, *not good enough* lack. This is where you *gasp*.

How many times has someone told you to be *realistic*? Which basically means, "Don't push the boat out, we've been told by our masters that there are demons in those waters."

It means keep your ideas small and work from within the 'box' and agree and behave within social convention.

And you try to, yet there is an area of your life where it is consistently accepted as 'realistic' to be dramatically, detrimentally and devastatingly unrealistic.

I don't know precisely what the reason is, but somehow everyone, even those with crippling confidence issues, self-esteem issues and other inhibiting beliefs akin to these seem to believe that they are superheroes who are just always underperforming.

When you don't meet your own expectations of what you are capable of, well, you've just purchased a one-way ticket to unhappy-ville haven't you? And yet this station seems to be the most visited destination in the universe.

This isn't to say that we should all under-expect of ourselves and wander the globe in a state of constant self-amazement. That too has its damaging sides. But actually, expecting anything at all could be a sure-fire way to ensure unhappiness.

Expecting a certain thing to be a certain way, or you to be able to do a certain thing to a certain level in a certain moment is lunacy. As we have addressed countless times in this book, you know nothing of the future, and yet you expect to know what you can and will do in said future based on ideas from past events which were and never will be the same as the future event in many different ways and for many different reasons.

You will never meet any expectation dead on, you will always under or over hit the mark. And even when you over hit on your expectation and it feels good, you were wrong, and that feels not so good.

It's a wonderful way to strip any opportunity for

happiness from the bone too, expectancy. You have an incredible week at work where you achieve record targets and get on with everyone, but part of you is not as happy as you could be because you believe you could have done better.

Now you're creating an imaginary outcome in an imaginary place about something in the past that you cannot affect nor impact. Here you have a perfect opportunity to be happy and in this moment enjoy the wonderful things you have created, and you choose not to feel as good as you can.

Worse still, while you were doing all of those amazing things you weren't actually enjoying them in that moment as much as you could have been because you were thinking about your future targets and how you can do better, forgetting rule 101; you will always do what you believe is best for you, and that therefore means that you will always do your best, however that represents itself.

So.

Question 44: *In what ways does being unhappy and believing you have underachieved serve you?*

Question 45: *In what ways does being unhappy and believing you have underachieved not serve you?*

Remember, there is ALWAYS a benefit to everything that you do. There are reasons why you choose to be unhappy.

A common reason to be unhappy that is woven into personal expectancy is when you feel you cannot make those you care about happy.

That's a lovely one right, how selfless. You're unhappy because they are not. Maybe. Because a part of that unhappiness also usually comes from your perceived inability to make them happy.

Question 46: *How is it possible that with all of your superpowers you can't change that person's world in an instant and make it all better?*

Question 47: *How do you even know what impact you're not having on them just by doing what you are doing?*

Question 48: *If you weren't doing what you were/are doing, what ways do you believe this situation might be different?*

Question 49: *What if you died to your need to create expectations of things. And everything that was, was,* and is, is and what will be, will be. And you are just the lucky person who gets to experience them as they come? In what ways would your life be different?

Question 50: *How much happier could you be if you didn't expect anything of yourself, and you just knew that everyday you are doing the best you can whether you think about it and analyse it and judge it or not? In what ways would your life be different?*

Of course expectancy doesn't just end at us. We expect a great deal of things from other people, both positive and negative and these expectations are no less unrealistic.

We meet people and decide things about them based on assumptions and prejudicial estimations.
We ignore all of the things we understand about human

capabilities and we believe that, like us, everyone else is a superhuman who is just underperforming.

These expectations will affect every microsecond of your communications and interactions. The way you expect someone to be will inform the way you respond. For example, if someone looks like a dangerous and *'threatening'* kind of person to you, yet they're softly spoken and seemingly very pleasant. It would directly conflict with your preconceived idea that they are a murderous psychopath, but even then as a result, because of the juxtaposition between what you expected of them and what you're experiencing of them, the likelihood is that you won't act comfortably and pleasantly back. If anything, it could be a ploy on their behalf to lull you into a false sense of security before all of the murdering happens, right?

Question 51: *If from now you chose not to expect*

others to be a certain way before you interact with them, what ways do you believe this would impact your interactions and your experience of those people?

Question 52: *What if by expecting others to be a certain way, your behaviour towards them as a result actually brings that out in them and you create the very thing you expected?*

You can see that even with the potential positives and 'negatives' associated with expectancy, it's a powerful thing and could easily become a minefield of drama, unwanted experiences and unhappiness.

Experiment 9:

For this experiment you will remove your judgement of others even if you already know the person. In doing so you will eliminate a large amount of your expectancy for them, how they will make you feel and the situations that might occur as a result of that person being around.

Then with every other area of your life, remove expectancy. This means that the moment you realise that you are expecting something, you stop and remind yourself, "Anything could happen. This doesn't have to be the way I am imagining it."

It is not always easy or obvious to clock when your expectancy of others and things is active, but there are some tell-tale signs.

If you enter a new situation or someone enters the

current situation and you feel any change. You have an expectancy. If you meet a new person and you think they look like a certain type of person, part of you expects that they will act in a way that agrees with that. This isn't to say let yourself get hurt recklessly, they may just be a bad egg as you predicted, but notice where you are making judgements and expecting something and cut it. Give everything including a new person an opportunity to be something you had never expected by expecting nothing.

The second part of this experiment, and potentially the most challenging part is giving yourself a break and cutting your expectations of yourself. Remember, you, like everyone else, are human. While you would love to believe you can do an additional eight-hours work in a normal working day simply because you are that efficient and fast, when that doesn't happen, give yourself a break and reassess exactly what you were expecting of yourself.

Aim high, but remember you ALWAYS do your best. You can't be and give more than 100% of *you* at any given time. How you choose to distribute that 100% is always in aim of creating your greatest perceived benefit.

The biggest benefits from this experiment come from slicing down negative expectations so if you prefer, start with your focus solely on these.

Again, this is a skill that will take time and practise. Test it and record your findings.

Fig 10: Draw an unexpected picture with something in it you wouldn't expect.

There's Nothing Wrong With
A Bit Of Self-Love

Question 53: *How would it be if you were more self-compassionate. If you stopped giving yourself such a hard time. If you stopped and appreciated all of the wonderful things that you have achieved in your life, and you admired if even for one second the person you are right now? How exactly would being more self-compassionate impact your life and the lives of those around you?*

How would that be? Probably very weird right? Because how often do you actually do that?

Let's be honest here. Even the most hardy of people can at points get hurt by things that others say if they take it personally. But in actual fact, what others say to you has nothing on the kind of awful things you say to yourself on a daily basis. I mean, if anyone spoke to you and behaved towards you in the way that you do to yourself, you'd be challenging them to duels, fisticuffs and have the police on speed dial.

Humans are wonderful at treating themselves awfully and being inwardly judgemental. I mean, just look at this stuff we say on a daily basis to ourselves:

- That was stupid
- I'm such an idiot
- I'm fat
- I'm ugly
- I'm stupid
- No one likes me
- Why don't they like me? (as this assumes it's true)
- I can't do that
- I'm not good enough
- I'm not worth it

- Why should anyone love me

- There's no point to me even living

Even reading those phrases can make you feel depressed.

We explored acceptance earlier and addressed how it may be a difficult thing to do, yet here we have a huge list of horrible things we say to ourselves that we accept willingly.

Question 54: *What are the benefits to you in accepting these 'stories' and believing them?*

Question 55: *What are the reasons behind why you find it as easy as you do to believe and accept these awful ideas about yourself?*

Question 56: *In what ways do you believe these reasons can be used to accept the other ideas, experiences and people as expressed in this book?*

Question 57: *In what ways do you believe these reasons to not be applicable to accepting other ideas, experiences and people as expressed in this book?*

Perhaps in answering this, you may discover the key to why you believed it would be so difficult to accept other areas of your life and live more positively. Perhaps also then you will give yourself permission to unlock those limiting beliefs to make living with more consistent happiness easier for you to access.

You now have another experiment to engage with.

Experiment 10:

Write down all of the things that you say to yourself that you wouldn't like others to say to you. This is going to be a progressive exercise and you should keep adding to this as you create new *'stories'*.

After you have written as many as you can recall, on a new page (or pages depending on how horrible you are to yourself) write down the most accurate opposite to each point that you can.

Every morning when you get up, before you do anything else. Read your new list and reread it until you feel as if you have understood and internalised your new points.

Each night before you go to bed, do the same thing and in your daily diary, note any changes that you have noticed as a result.

At The End Of The Day

It has been scientifically documented, numerously, that we internalise things during sleep that we engaged with shortly beforehand.

It is partly why your daily diary and experiments such as 10 include a night-time activity.

Experiment 11:

As well as reading your list of anti-abuse each night, you are going to practise being present. That means bringing your mind, your thoughts and your attention to right now.

As part of your diary commitments you will explore how in this moment you are really feeling, and also practise gratitude.

You and I might have never met, though I hope we do. But I already know that you have so many wonderful things in your life that sometimes it is easy for you to take them for granted, or even forget they exist at all amongst the bigger and more obvious things in your life. Those which probably aren't so enjoyable.

Right now is your moment to be grateful.

In order to do this with full effect, first give yourself a moment to clear your mind so all that you are doing is breathing in, and breathing out.

To start with, clearing your mind won't be easy. You will think things, particularly things such as, "Oh no, I'm thinking." And that's okay. Don't panic and get yourself into a cycle of think, panic, think, panic, give up, panic... Recognise that you thought what you thought and let it go as easily as it came.

As with the other skills that you have been learning from this book, this will get easier with practice. Buddhist monks have practiced 'empty mind' meditation for centuries (an extreme version of what you are doing right now) and far from making them vacant, it provides them an opportunity to silence mental chatter and thus offer up moments of crystallising clarity. If anything, it is worth practising this simply in hope that you too one day will be able to break steel bars on your head and levitate!

Clearing your mind to do this experiment is best done with no time pressures, but this I understand isn't always available to you. One thing you can do if you have time restrictions is set an alarm for when you want to stop. Make this at least 10 minutes though! This way you free up that clock-watching part of your mind and enable yourself to chill. Once the rush-hour traffic in your head has calmed, we can begin.

Think of one single thing that you, in this exact moment, are grateful for.

Once you have that, make it as bold and as vivid as you can. If you are a visual person, increase the vibrancy, the brightness, the boldness of the colours. Imagine the thing that you are grateful for and picture yourself being and feeling grateful for that.

If you are an auditory person, give what you are grateful for a sound, make it clear, let the sound resonate with your feeling of gratefulness. Hear yourself being grateful for it, and feel inside as if you were with that which you are grateful.

If you are a kinaesthetic person, imagine you are touching and feeling that which you are grateful for. If it is intangible, make it tangible. If you could feel it, what would it feel like? Feel yourself being grateful for that.

In your diary, add what it is that you are grateful for. Tomorrow you will be grateful for something new. You will never run out, and that is a wonderful thing to know.

While you are still relatively calm, you are going to do one final thing. I mentioned at the very beginning of this book about engaging with emotional check-ins and clocking your happiness gauge and you were tasked with, "...locking-down in your mind what exactly happiness is to you and what it would look like and feel like to be at the baseline of your happiness."

I will say this like one of those scary teachers who is using mind-control tricks, "I know you have done this." To let you know that if you haven't, now would be a good time to do so!

Now that you know what it would look like and feel like for you to be at your baseline of happiness, you are in a great position to understand more clearly how you are feeling in any given moment, at least in relation to that place where you want to come from – happiness.

Once in the morning, once during the day and once before bed. Ask yourself:

Question 58: *What am I feeling right now in this precise moment?*

Just a note here, it is best to give yourself specific times to do this. The reason for this is because whenever something happens that you are not happy with you will think of all the ways that you can cement that unhappiness and justify it and make it bigger and more dominant in your mind. Though you may not be aware you are doing this at the time, the moment you feel unhappy will most likely be the exact moment you think, *ping* (that's the light bulb above your head) I feel a strong emotion, I can do my check-in.

Not only will this result in a daily list of bad feelings to mull over, but it won't give a fair and accurate representation of your actual life. Moreover, this experiment isn't designed to clock 'strong' feelings; if anything it is designed to highlight the opposite. To bring greater emotional awareness to the moments where you believe either you don't know what you feel or you feel nothing at all.

Choose a time, keep it regular and commit to that. No matter what. Deal?

The second part of this experiment goes like this.

In answering question 58, you will describe to yourself everything you are experiencing via your thoughts and feelings in this precise moment. After you have done this. Write down your findings in your diary and continue with your day. If you do not wish to carry such a valuable and personal item with you throughout the day, take note of your findings in whatever way you can and add them that day to your diary for your scientific records.

The experiment doesn't exist to give you data to analyse over a set period of time. Doing so could be hazardous depending on the way you choose to analyse these results.

The purpose of engaging with the final part of this experiment is to increase your own personal awareness and debunk this idea of you being generally unhappy, by bringing more clearly to your mind exactly how you are feeling. Frequent check-ins will start to build habitual pathways and connections in your mind and over time you will become more emotionally aware more of the time without having to focus on it.

Knowing what you believe it would feel and look like to be at your baseline level of happiness will additionally act as a good gauge of where you are at.

If in that moment you are not at least at that level, you have in this book all of the resources you require to help you understand why that might be, and how exactly you can change that.

Fig 11: Draw what you are grateful for in this moment.

On Your Bike

How I would love to say, "You are done!" right now. I could, but I would be lying.

In truth you will never really be done. In engaging with this book, you have adopted a range of new ways to actively live a happier, and therefore, better life. You have also displaced many of the ways that weren't positively contributing to the life you want to lead, so you don't have to worry about being overrun with too much 'stuff' to maintain. You do the same amount already, the difference is that the things that you do now are not all in favour of your happiness. In order to make sure that you don't feel exhausted and overworked; which is easy to feel, not because you have more things to do, but actually because of how uncomfortable the change is from your old lifestyle, you will benefit from progressively removing more of the behaviours that are no longer serving you in creating the life you want to lead.

Right now this may work for you, but if it feels like removing negative pathways is just adding to your workload, you may benefit from slowing things down. Remember, what you are doing with this book is remapping and reprogramming your brain and changing many of the behaviours and habits that you have developed and refined over many years. Be okay with the process taking time, it took a long time for you to get to how you are now. Be self-compassionate and know that beating yourself up will slow down your growth and directly impede your ability to create your own happiness, as doing so actively manufactures the opposite.

The birth of this transition as with all births will be messy, confusing, exhausting and at points you'll probably want to give up. Please don't.

The things you now know and have learnt and have

committed to experimenting with are gifts. Use them as best you can to lead the most fulfilled, enjoyable and happy life you never dreamt possible. This is, I must admit, for my own selfish reasons because I would love for you to be happy. But in the end, only you can choose however you want to live. Your final task is this:

Use everything you have learnt and maintain the experiments you have committed to, to inform your re-reading of this book.

That's right. Re-read this book.

You may see things differently this time, and the experiments that you are currently running may throw forward some interesting results as a consequence.

It can be difficult to begin new things by yourself, diets for instance can die fast when you aren't regularly hearing the stories of Fat-Mary's midnight kitchen rampages. And when you don't have others holding you accountable, and who aren't looking to you for accountability, it is far easier to get caught-up in the busy and stressful life you chose to live before reading this book that you were not happy living.

So share your stories of this book, share what you are learning, heck, even do it with others and bounce off each other's happiness (this by the way is another wonderful way to feel great.)

For now, I will see you later. Outside of these pages I love taking people on adventures and helping them transform their lives, their careers and businesses.

I work with top performers and high-achievers to bring out their greatest results.

If you want to grow and develop and create a better

way for you or others in an unimaginable way, and love the idea of an adventure, both physical and metaphorical), you know where I am.

If you are a manager or a business owner who wants to create a more cohesive, creative, enjoyable and effective working environment. You know where I am.

If you are an entrepreneur and you want help to turn your explosive passion into a laser focused energy. You know where I am.

And if you simply want more from life and want to explore how you can have that. You know where I am.

Until then. Take risks and scuff your knees a little.

Skyler

P.S. Why not continue the conversation online? There are many other people who want what you want and there are some interesting ways for you to share your experiences. Why not send in your stories, pictures you have drawn for the book and even your scientific findings from your experiments to the social media links below!

www.skylershah.co.uk

@SkylerShah #FullOfHappiness

Facebook.com/groups/APocketFullOfHappiness

www.skylershah.co.uk

@SkylerShah #FullOfHappiness

Facebook.com/groups/**APocketFullOfHappiness**

List Of Questions

Question 1: *What are the mental and real-world physical consequences of me being unhappy with this?*

Question 2: *How do I benefit from this?*

Question 3: *If instead of being unhappy I was happy, it would not be beneficial for me because it would mean...*

Question 4: *What difference would it make, from today, if I no longer believed that I was bad at making decisions?*

Question 5: *What are my reasons for why, this time, have I chosen to believe that I am bad at making decisions? How does this belief benefit me?*

Question 6: *What exactly am I afraid of happening as a result or in the process of confidently making a decision?*

Question 7: *What is the worst-case scenario possible as a result of me not acting on my belief that I am bad at making decisions?*

Question 8: *What is the best-case scenario possible as a result of me not acting on my belief that I am bad at making decisions?*

Question 9: *What is the most probable outcome of me not acting on my belief that I am bad at making decisions? And how terrible, really, would that actually be in the scope of the entire wonderful life I have yet to live and create?*

Question 10: *What does it mean about who I am and how I am right now, that I felt/feel, thought/think,* responded/respond how I did/do? What else does it mean? (Keep asking that tag question until you feel you truly have nowhere else to go.)

Question 11: *If from today you chose to do what made you happy, in what ways could you not be making the 'wrong' decision?*

Question 12: *If from today you chose to do what made you happy, in what ways might you be making the 'wrong' decision?*

Question 13: *What could be possible if instead of trying to 'know' what to do with your life, you decided to 'be' in your life and by doing so, made each moment great for you?*

Question 14: *Imagine you have a completely clean and fresh canvas as your life. What would you love to do with it?*

Question 15: *What, from your vision in question 14, can you bring into your life today to help you begin that process of living into your dream?*

Question 16: *Am I prepared to love myself, to live congruently to who I am, even if it means that the relationships, things and people I love right now might change either by improving or ending, which too will be an improvement?*

Question 17: *Am I prepared to love those around me enough to let them experience me at my greatest and happiest, and love them no matter how they respond to that?*

Question 18: *What actually would doing the wrong thing look like to you?*

Question 19: *How would you know it was the 'wrong' thing?*

Question 20: *What are the definitive guidelines for you that in agreeing with, you would be doing the 'right' thing?*

Question 21: *What is your favourite colour, right now?*

Question 22: *Which items on the right-hand side of the page can you immediately cut out?*

Question 23: *Which items can you edit or change to make energising?*

Question 24: *Knowing that you choose to engage with all of the things that drain you that you believe you 'have to' and 'need to' engage with; what do you want to do about them, and how do you want to feel about them?*

Question 25: *In what ways specifically could your life be more amazing if you lived more in the left-hand* *side of your page?*

Question 26: *If as a result of you being congruent others are not happy. What does that mean to you?*

Question 27: *If as a result you being congruent others are not happy. What might it mean about them? (give more than one answer)*

Question 28: *To what extent would your world end if those who were unhappy with you being congruent weren't in your life?*

Question 29: *What could you do to help those who are unhappy with you being congruent to see how you now see?*

Question 30: *What would your life be like if you put all of your 'flaws' and problems, and areas where you are wonderful, and areas where you are a terrible human* *being, all out into the light and you just said:*

This is me. I don't have to like it, in fact I don't and there are some things now that I can clearly see in this light that I want to change. But right now this is me. And that is okay.

Question 31: *Every single second I have a fresh start and a choice. How do I choose to feel right now?*

Question 32: *Every single second I have a fresh start and a choice. How do I choose to live right now?*

Question 33: *Every single second I have a fresh start and a choice. Who, in this second, do I choose to be?*

Question 34: *I am worried about (state your worry.) I am fearful that this worry will come true because it will damage/ hurt/ kill/ I will lose/ I will not gain (state the things you are afraid of losing as a result of this worry's manifestation.) This worries me because (what* *that means to you.)*

Question 35: *What do I fear losing as a result of this imaginary scenario/set of scenarios coming true?*

Question 36: *What if you just knew that you did what you did, and that you are smart enough to be able to deal with anything that may happen in the future? What would be different?*

Question 37: *How could life be then for you?*

Question 38: *How would you feel and think differently about any given situation if you functioned from that place?*

Question 39: *What if by imagining all of the 'terrible' ways your life could end up, what if by simply entertaining those ideas as possibilities, you are in some way facilitating those existences into a potential* *reality of yours?*

Question 40: *What if by imagining that horrible outcome as a possibility, it actually becomes a possibility that you worry about, and then your actions start to direct you towards that as a result of your focus and attention?*

Question 41: *In what ways is this/ are these benefit(s) derived from fear?*

Question 42: *Am I going to choose to act out of fear and preservation? Am I going to admit and be accountable to myself that I am owned by my fears and sitting frightened in the passenger seat?*

Question 43: *Am I going to decide to take action against living those realities, and for a new more empowering one. To sit at the wheel and own everything that is me, including my fears?*

Question 44: *In what ways does being unhappy and believing you have underachieved serve you?*

Question 45: *In what ways does being unhappy and believing you have underachieved not serve you?*

Question 46: *How is it possible that with all of your superpowers you can't change that person's world in an instant and make it all better?*

Question 47: *How do you even know what impact you're not having on them just by doing what you are doing?*

Question 48: *If you weren't doing what you were/are doing, what ways do you believe this situation might be different?*

Question 49: *What if you died to your need to create expectations of things. And everything that was, was,* and is, is and what will be, will be. And you are just the lucky person who gets to experience them as they come? In what ways would your life be different?

Question 50: How much happier could you be if you didn't expect anything of yourself, and you just knew that everyday you are doing the best you can whether you think about it and analyse it and judge it or not? In what ways would your life be different?

Question 51: If from now you chose not to expect others to be a certain way before you interact with them, what ways do you believe this would impact your interactions and your experience of those people?

Question 52: What if by expecting others to be a certain way, your behaviour towards them as a result actually brings that out in them and you create the very thing you expected?

Question 53: *How would it be if you were more self-compassionate. If you stopped giving yourself such a hard time. If you stopped and appreciated all of the wonderful things that you have achieved in your life, and you admired if even for one second the person you are right now? How exactly would being more self-compassionate impact your life and the lives of those around you?*

Question 54: *What are the benefits to you in accepting these 'stories' and believing them?*

Question 55: *What are the reasons behind why you find it as easy as you do to believe and accept these awful ideas about yourself?*

Question 56: *In what ways do you believe these reasons can be used to accept the other ideas, experiences and people as expressed in this book?*

Question 57: *In what ways do you believe these reasons to not be applicable to accepting other ideas, experiences and people as expressed in this book?*

Question 58: *What am I feeling right now in this precise moment?*

www.skylershah.co.uk

@SkylerShah #FullOfHappiness

Facebook.com/groups/**APocketFullOfHappiness**

www.skylershah.co.uk

@SkylerShah #FullOfHappiness

Facebook.com/groups/**APocketFullOfHappiness**

55371993R00128

Made in the USA
Charleston, SC
26 April 2016